SOIL,
SOUL,
SOCIETY

OTHER BOOKS BY SATISH KUMAR

Earth Pilgrim

Elegant Simplicity: The Art of Living Well

No Destination: Autobiography of a Pilgrim

Pilgrimage for Peace: The Long Walk from India to Washington

Radical Love: From Separation to Connection with the Earth, Each Other, and Ourselves

Regenerative Learning: Education as if People and Planet Matter

Small World, Big Ideas: Eco-Activists for Change

Spiritual Compass: The Three Qualities of Life

Transformative Learning: : Reflections on Thirty Years of Head, Heart, and Hands at Schumacher College

You Are, Therefore I Am: A Declaration of Dependence

SOIL,
SOUL,
SOCIETY

A New Trinity for Our Time

SATISH KUMAR

Foreword by Marion Cotillard

Introduction by Lindsay Clarke

PARALLAX PRESS
BERKELEY, CALIFORNIA

Parallax Press
2236B Sixth Street
Berkeley, CA 94710
parallax.org

Parallax Press is the publishing division of
Plum Village Community of Engaged Buddhism, Inc

First published in the UK by Leaping Hare Press in 2013

UK edition published in 2023 by The Resurgence Trust. Books by Satish Kumar
are available in the UK from *www.resurgence.org/books*.

Extracts from *Purbi: A Miscellany, Correspondence between Tagore and Leonard
Elmhirst* reproduced by kind permission of Dartington Hall Trust. Extracts from
I Won't Let You Go, Selected Poems by Rabindranath Tagore reproduced by kind
permission of Ketaki Dyson and Bloodaxe Books.

Cover art and cover design by Jess Morphew
Text design by Maureen Forys, Happenstance Type-O-Rama
Author photograph by Geoff Dalglish

Printed in the United States of America by Versa Press
Printed on recycled paper

Library of Congress Control Number: 2024940077

1 2 3 4 5 VERSA 29 28 27 26 25 24

To my friends and hosts
James and Margaret Sainsbury

CONTENTS

FOREWORD

To educate myself; to awaken my conscience; to face up to my responsibilities; to engage; to defend causes, both beautiful and meaningful; to strive to reduce any negative impacts of my actions on this Earth, which supports me and gives me everything; to do my best to preserve it.

For many years, I spoke with conviction about the harmony and peace that this planet needs and of the love this magnificent and generous Earth deserves.

Yet when I found myself alone, I was incapable of finding harmony and peace within myself. Incapable of looking at myself with love. So, I threw myself at all available means of escape, of which we have created so many.

I put so much energy into defending the planet, into behaving in an exemplary manner. However, at the same time, I was happily polluting the first natural home I had: myself.

One day, I came across this simple sentence: "The best project you can work on is yourself." This interested me deeply and sparked the beginnings of a great internal tumult.

I've always thought that the world mirrors what we carry within ourselves. So I faced my inner discomfort. I started to examine my conscience more intimately and much more subtly than I ever had before.

All the action I had taken for the planet had of course been useful and constructive, but now it was time for me to connect on another level with the purity of the nature we are part of and that is part of us.

With the purity of my most profound being.

With the silence. The true silence. To no longer allow myself to be invaded by thoughts, most of which were useless and vain. To free up space within me for a sustainable evolution. And to stand by my convictions.

It wasn't always easy. Certain readings and encounters guided me along the way. The most magical and wonderful part of this process of internal "decluttering" was how life sends us exactly what we need. Satish Kumar is one of those messengers. His outlook, his love, his simplicity, and his logic showed me the power I held within myself. The connection I reestablished with my internal home and my soul gave a new quality to my relationship with society and evolution within it. A new vibration with the present moment. A clearer vision of the things that surround us.

What touches me the most about Satish Kumar's words is that they reconnect what our society has wrongly divided. He reveals that this internal home within us, the cradle of our soul, and the external natural home that supports us are intrinsically linked. This connection is essential for harmony and peace to emerge. By taking care of ourselves, we take care of others and of the natural world around us. Taking care of the Earth is an inspiration and a true message of love for ourselves.

He delivers a great message of peace.

I am a being under construction, I still have a long path ahead of me, but it is with great joy that, every day, I discover what gifts await me on that path. This book is one of them.

MARION COTILLARD

SATISH KUMAR

A Man of Courage and Imagination

For more than twenty years now, Satish Kumar has been one of my most valued friends, not only because of his own warm, inspirational nature, but also because of the number of other visionaries to whom I've been introduced through working with him at Schumacher College and elsewhere.

Among those distinguished radical thinkers was the archetypal psychologist James Hillman, whose marvelous book *The Soul's Code* promotes the understanding that we do not come into this world as a blank slate, but with intimations of who we already are and what our life is meant to be about. In support of his thesis, Hillman quotes many convincing examples of people whose destinies were shaped by such intuitive knowledge, but it seems to me that he need have looked no further for conclusive proof of the truth of his thesis than in the life of his friend Satish.

Why else, I wonder, should a nine-year-old boy in Rajasthan have told his family that the time had come for him to leave home and join the Jain Monks who, in their absolute reverence for life, are among the strictest of all spiritual orders, unless he already knew it his duty to become a Pilgrim of the Earth? How else to explain the promptings of the inner voice which told Satish, when he was eighteen and aware of the suffering and injustice in the world, to leave that mendicant order and follow the teachings of Mahatma Gandhi by joining Vinoba Bhave's nonviolent campaign for land reform in India?

How else to account for the fact that in 1962 Bertrand Russell's campaign for nuclear disarmament inspired Satish and his friend E.P. Menon to walk, without a penny in their pockets, on a pilgrimage for peace from New Delhi to Moscow, Paris, London, and Washington, carrying a packet of peace tea for each leader of the four nuclear powers with the advice that, before resorting to nuclear warfare as a solution to their problems, they should sit down and have a quiet cup of tea? And then, how else to account for the fact that when he came to the UK in 1973, this sprightly idealist from such humble beginnings should quickly establish himself as one of the most serious and significant voices in the land?

Satish Kumar is clearly a man who has honored with exemplary courage and imagination the special destiny that brought him into this life. He has won an international reputation as the editor of *Resurgence*, the magazine which for decades now has been the most articulate champion of ecological awareness, of social and economic justice, and of a reverent way of life characterized by a philosophy of non-violence and humane spiritual values. By starting The Small School in Hartland, he created a model for imaginative community education; as the energetic founding Director of Schumacher College, he has brought some of the world's most important thinkers and activists to teach while playing his own vital role in the evolution of consciousness happening in our time.

Out of his passionate care for the life of this beautiful planet we harm in so many destructive ways, Satish Kumar has long been a tireless campaigner for issues of urgent importance. Whether as editor, educator, writer, or speaker on radio and television, his life and work are a vital demonstration of what can be achieved when our sense of the world and our activities within it are reinvested with the healing and transformative powers of the soul. Those powers will be found, excitingly alive and well, within the pages of this book.

LINDSAY CLARKE

PREFACE
TO THE 2024 EDITION

Soil is the source of all life, literally and metaphorically. All life comes from mother soil and returns to her. I love the soil as my mother and take care of her. Soil contains the elements of earth, air, fire, and water. She is nature herself.

If my outer body is soil, then my inner being is the soul. As I cultivate the soil to grow food for the body, I take care of the soul and cultivate love, compassion, beauty, and unity to realize harmony within and without.

When I am at ease within, I am at ease without. I am at ease with the whole of humanity. Through caring for soil, I am a member of the Earth community, and through caring for society, I am a member of the human community. Billions of people, with their diversities of cultures and colors, are one human family. I suffer with their suffering and I rejoice in their happiness. The trinity of Soil, Soul, Society is a way of saying in three words that we are all related, interconnected, and interdependent. This is a trinity of wholeness and unity of life in its myriad forms.

I am delighted that this new edition of *Soil, Soul, Society* is being published by Parallax Press, which was cofounded by the great teacher of interdependence Thich Nhat Hanh, a guiding light and a source of inspiration to me over a long period of my life. I first met Thay, as I call him (the Vietnamese word for "teacher") and Sister Chan Khong in Paris in 1968, where they had taken refuge after being exiled from their home country of Vietnam for their antiwar activities. The peace movement at that time in Europe and America was fervently engaged in stopping the war in Vietnam. For us nonviolent peace activists, Thay was the voice of spiritual and radical wisdom. For him, peace in Vietnam was related to peace in the entire world, within and without. He reminded us again and again that to make peace, we have to "*Be* peace!"

Because of his holistic vision of comprehensive peace, Thay was invited to speak at the first-ever United Nations Conference on the Human Environment in Stockholm in 1972. I had the privilege to be there with him, and listening to his profound insights, I was reminded of Mahatma Gandhi. I felt that Thay was the Gandhi of our time. So, when I organized the Sarvodaya Conference in London in 1975, I thought of Thay as a star speaker, and invited him to travel from Paris for this historic occasion. (The word *sarvodaya*, coined by Gandhi, means the well-being of humans and more.) The sarvodaya ideal proposes that to achieve political peace, we also need an economy of peace. E. F. Schumacher, whom I write about at length in this book, had just published his book *Small Is Beautiful*, in which there is a chapter on Buddhist economics. Schumacher was delighted to meet Thay, and together they held a fruitful dialogue about Buddhism, economics, and peace.

Even in those early years, Thay was an embodiment of love and compassion. To him, ecological, spiritual, and social issues were indistinguishable. Knowing that I am a Gandhian and peace activist, he said to me, "To make peace in the world, we have to make peace with ourselves and peace with Nature!" This became my mantra, the seeds of the idea of a new trinity for our time in the form of Soil, Soul, Society. Eventually, I discovered that Hindu philosophy also endorsed similar ideas as Buddhism, as did Jain philosophy. It was a beautiful confluence of these three spiritual traditions of India as well as the work of three contemporary visionaries—Gandhi, E. F. Schumacher, and Thay—that brought me to seek out this holistic trinity for our time, which has finally emerged in this book.

Mahayana Buddhism sees that we are all related: no one can be enlightened by oneself until all living beings are enlightened. We are all interdependent beings, *interbeing*. There is no separation between nature and humans. There is no separation between humans in the name of religion, race, color, or nationality. Life is a continuum. The diversity of life is rooted in the unity of life; we celebrate diversity as well as unity. Unity is not uniformity and diversity is not division; unity and diversity dance together. Nature, spirit, and human community, in other words Soil, Soul, and Society, are interlinked. This wisdom is at the core of the Buddhist philosophy that has been highlighted by Plum Village, the community in France established by Thich Nhat Hanh. It has been my honor and pleasure to be associated with Plum Village all these years and continue to engage in this living dialogue with the wise monastics and lay people there.

If we look deeply and understand the essence of all wisdom traditions and spiritual beliefs, we will realize that caring for the Earth and caring for one other is at the core of all religious teachings. But under the influence of mechanistic materialism, we have lost our spiritual values and religious principles of reverence for all life. Our educational system and scientific materialism lead us to look at the soil and see it as soulless, to perceive Nature as a machine and merely a commodity, a resource for the economy. This world view has led us to exploit Nature, resulting in the loss of biodiversity and climate catastrophe.

The worldview presented in this book celebrates the living soil and holds that soil is soulful. Nature all together is a living organism. This planet, our common home, is not a dead rock; she is Gaia, Earth Goddess. If we sincerely and seriously wish to solve the urgent problem of climate catastrophe, then we need to restore our reverence for soil, our love for Nature, and our gratitude to the living planet. This book is a humble effort to encourage us to do exactly that.

There is no separation between soil, soul, and society, between ecological integrity, spiritual fulfillment, and social harmony. We share one Earth, one humanity, and one future. These are three dimensions of a new, holistic paradigm, which reminds us to expand our view beyond our narrow boundaries, identities, and experience:

> The whole cosmos as our country.
> The whole Earth as our home.
> Nature as our nationality.
> And love as our religion.

This is what I have learned from Thay, from Plum Village, and from the timeless teachings of the Buddha, as well as Gandhi, Tagore, and E. F. Schumacher, to whom I pay tribute in these pages. I am honored to present these teachings in my own words through this book. Enjoy!

SATISH KUMAR
Hartland, Devon
May 2024

INTRODUCTION

The trinity of Soil, Soul, Society is a distillation of much learning and living. Born and brought up in India for the first half of my life and then living in the West for the second half, I have gained much from both worlds, for which I am grateful.

While reading *Talks on the Gita* by Vinoba Bhave, I came across a concept articulated in three Sanskrit words that gave me a way of understanding and establishing a right relationship with nature, the self, and society. These words were *yagna, tapas, dana,* or sacrifice, generosity, and self-discipline.

Then, while walking from New Delhi to Moscow, Paris, London, and Washington for the cause of peace, I realized that peace is not just an absence of war; rather it is a way of being in harmony with planet Earth, with oneself, and with all human beings on the planet irrespective of their race, religion, or nationality. That long walk became my meditation on the reality of interdependence and interbeing.

I have studied Buddhist philosophy from a very early age, but only when I reflected on the teachings of the Buddha within the context of the interrelatedness of planet, person, and people did I understand the deep meaning of the four noble truths—which, I realized, are a means of healing the Earth, the soul, and society. There can be no healing of the self if the Earth around us is sick and human communities are suffering.

In my youth I was a Jain monk and learned the principles of nonviolence, self-restraint, and self-discipline, but at that time I looked at these principles only from the point of view of personal liberation. However, studying the Bhagavad Gita and walking through many cultures and examining the profound meaning of the four noble truths in my meditation, I saw the Jain principles in a different light. Doing no harm and practicing nonviolence toward plants, animals, and people was at once a way of enhancing my relationship with the natural world, the inner world, and the social world. If our civilization were to embrace nonviolence, self-restraint, and self-discipline, we would avoid ecological calamities, personal alienation, and social injustice.

The Jain word as well as the word used in the Gita for self-discipline is *tapas*, which is related to heat, and I found this most interesting. Once, Vinoba explained that when fruit ripens in the heat of the sun it gains a beautiful color, a delightful aroma, and a delicious taste because the fruit has gone through the heat of the sun. So, if you wish to gain ripeness and sweetness, you also have to go through the heat of self-discipline. Even grains and vegetables ripened by the sun need to go through the heat of the stove to become edible and digestible. Metaphorically, such food is making *tapas*.

Another example is gold; to transform a bar of gold into wearable jewelry, gold has to go through the heat of fire. And clay must go through the heat of the kiln to become a usable pot. Unless we practice self-discipline, we cannot transform ourselves from being to becoming. All spiritual practices are forms of self-discipline to strengthen the soul and to make the self resilient for all eventualities.

Mahatma Gandhi set a supreme example of self-discipline as well as the practice of self-restraint and nonviolence. He presented a trinity of his own, which is very similar to the trinity of Soil, Soul, Society. Throughout my life, Gandhi has been a guiding light. Whether implicitly or explicitly, he insisted upon reverence for all living beings, human and other-than-human. He always made time for a personal practice of meditation, silence, prayers, and fasting for the care of his soul. And then he devoted his life's work to uplifting the poor, the untouchables, the downtrodden, and the deprived. For all these reasons, Gandhian ideas are essential to presenting the trinity of Soil, Soul, Society.

While Gandhi's life provided the fertile ground for my trinity, Rabindranath Tagore set the scene through poetry. Politics without poetry is incomplete. Ever since I came across the stories, songs, paintings, plays, and poetry of Tagore, I became enthralled by the power of his imagination. We will be ill-equipped to care for the soil, nourish the soul, and nurture society without the power of imagination manifested through the enchantment of poetry, the spell of songs. The trinity of Soil, Soul, Society is very much inspired by the poetry of Tagore.

Tagore was not only a poet, he was also a great educator. He started a school as well as a university. He held classes under trees and said to his pupils, "You have two teachers: me, a human teacher, and the tree, under which we sit, your nature teacher. You can learn much more wisdom from the tree than from me." Tagore was so right. And who can equal the generosity of a tree? A tree gives its fruit unconditionally to anyone and everyone.

Tagore's school became an inspiration to me for starting The Small School in Hartland, where I live, as well as Schumacher College at Dartington, both in Devon. In these educational experiments I have broadened the focus. Rather than emphasizing reading, writing, and arithmetic (the three Rs), we emphasize head, heart, and hands (the three Hs).

My life as a Jain monk, a walker for peace, a student of Buddhist philosophy, a worker in the Gandhian movement, and a follower of the wisdom of Tagore introduced me to the ideals of the East. Then I met E. F. Schumacher, a Western economist, environmentalist, philosopher, and practitioner of spiritual disciplines. E. F. Schumacher embodied the ideals of Soil, Soul, Society. If I had to name one book from the West that has molded my thinking most, then that would be Schumacher's *Small Is Beautiful*. When world trends were moving toward centralization, globalization, militarization, and commercialization, Schumacher had the courage and audacity to speak for a local, self-reliant, ecological, spiritual, simple, nonviolent, and elegant way of life. These values and the living example of Schumacher himself have informed my writing and editing.

Much of my writing has been to illuminate the philosophy of wholeness and the articulation of Soil, Soul, Society. This book is a way of acknowledging my debt to these teachers and activists and paying my tribute and gratitude to their inspiring work.

1

Soil, Soul, Society

I put soil first because it represents nature and sustains the entire life system. Everything comes from the soil and returns to the soil.

Great movements and perennial philosophies throughout history have often summarized their essential message in three words, a trinity. One of the Hindu trinities is Brahman, Vishnu, and Shiva—the principles of creation, continuity, and decay, or in other words, birth, life, and death. Christians have the Father, the Son, and the Holy Spirit. The Greeks focused on Truth, Goodness, and Beauty.

The writers of the American Constitution came up with Life, Liberty, and the Pursuit of Happiness. The French Revolution with Liberty, Equality, and Fraternity. In our own time, the New Age movement gathered around the concepts of Mind, Body, and Spirit. These trinities have their point and are relevant in their own context—but none of them represents a holistic and ecological world view in an explicit manner. They are either spiritual or social, but they are mostly anthropocentric and fail to highlight our relationship with nature or the connection between the social and the spiritual.

I came across three words in an ancient Hindu text, the Bhagavad Gita, that stimulated my thinking on ecology, spirituality, and humanity. Those three words in Sanskrit are *yagna*, *tapas*, and *dana*. *Yagna* informs human/nature relationships, *tapas* relates to inner dimension, and *dana* relates to social relationships. I have translated and interpreted this trinity as Soil, Soul, Society.

Care of the Soil

I put soil first because it represents nature and sustains the entire life system. Everything comes from the soil and

8

returns to the soil. Food, which sustains life, comes from the soil. Water, which nourishes life, is held by the soil. The sun, the moon, and the stars all relate to the soil. The soil is a metaphor for the entire natural system. If we take care of the soil, the soil will take care of us all. Through the soil we are all related and interconnected. We are held and sustained by the soil. We depend on the soil. All living beings depend on the soil, and soil treats all living beings equally. Rich or poor, poet or peasant, young or old, whoever we are, soil loves us all unconditionally and feeds us all indiscriminately.

> *Hope is the thing with feathers*
> *That perches in the soul*
> *And sings the tune without words*
> *And never stops at all*
>
> EMILY DICKINSON

Unfortunately, the sciences, technology, economics, and philosophy have developed in such a way in the past few centuries that we have elevated humankind to the ruling position and given humans higher status than all other beings. We have developed a world view that dictates that the human species is superior to all other species. Animals, forests, rivers, and oceans must serve and fulfill not only the needs of humankind but also its greed and desires. This way of thinking has been called speciesism, which means that one species, the human species, is the superior species above all others.

This arrogant world view has led to the demise of reciprocal, mutual, respectful, reverential, and spiritual relationships between humans and the rest of nature. In fact, humans have come to believe that they are separate from nature and above nature. Nature is out *there*: the forests, the rivers, the birds, and other wildlife, and we humans are *here*, enclosed in our homes, palaces, castles, apartments, offices, cars, trains, and airplanes.

In the recent past, there have been philosophers and scientists who have considered it right for humanity to go on a mission of conquering nature through technology, science, industry, and trade. Humanity has been at war against nature during this industrial and technological age, poisoning the land with chemicals and pesticides in the name of increasing food production. We have put birds and animals in coops and cages and treated them cruelly so that greater and greater profit can be made through increased sales of animal protein; relentless destruction of rainforest as well as deciduous forest has been justified to increase areas of arable land for agribusiness; the industrial scale of fishing is another example of our acts of war against nature. Little do we realize that even if we were to win the war, we would find ourselves on the losing side.

This war against nature is driven by our conviction that the function of nature is to fuel the engine of the economy. But the truth of the matter is that the economy is a wholly owned subsidiary of ecology. If the natural capital is depleted, the natural environment is destroyed, and the economy will come to an end!

Thus, the challenge for humankind in the twenty-first century is to find humility and reconnect with nature. We need to understand that nature is not just "out there"; we are nature too. The word "nature" means birth. "Natal," "nativity," "native," and "nature" all come from the same root. Whatever is born and will die is nature. Since we humans are also born and will die, we are nature, too. Nature and humans are one. Therefore, we need to understand that what we do to nature we do to ourselves. If we harm nature, we harm ourselves. We are all related; we live in an interdependent world.

With this sense of the unity of humans and nature, we come to a new way of appreciating and valuing all life. The Norwegian philosopher Arne Naess called it "deep ecology." When we value nature only in terms of her usefulness to humans, even if we conserve her and protect her for our benefit, it is shallow ecology; when we recognize the intrinsic value of all life, small or large, then it is deep ecology. A blade of grass, an earthworm, an insect, even a mosquito has the right to life; so do trees, rivers, birds, and fish, irrespective of their usefulness to humans.

Deep ecology emerges out of deep experience of nature. Our modern way of life lacks that deep experience because we hardly interact with nature. Our life is designed to keep us away from her. Our homes, our offices, our shops are completely disconnected from nature. Modern life is lived under artificial light, in air-conditioning, and moistened by bottled water!

To be able to have deep experience of nature, we have to touch the soil, walk in woods, swim in the sea, watch the clouds, and celebrate the sunset. Only from such deep experience can a deep commitment to respect and care for nature arise. Only then can we move from consumerism to conservation.

As we recognize human rights, deep ecology requires us to recognize the rights of nature. Our relationship with nature has to be embedded in the principles of reverence for life. Deep ecology leads to reverential and spiritual ecology. Nature is not a dead object. Nature is alive. The scientist James Lovelock has proposed the theory of Gaia, that the Earth is a living organism.

In Hindu philosophy, nature is considered to be intelligent and conscious. The elements earth, air, fire, and water have divinity intrinsic to them. Hindus talk about the rain god, Indra; the wind god, Vayu; the fire goddess, Agni; and the Earth goddess, Bhoomi. They also talk about the sun god; the moon goddess; the god of the Himalayas, Shiva; the goddess of water, Ganga. In essence, gods and goddesses are not separate from nature.

Commenting on the Gita, Vinoba Bhave says that all that is around us is nothing but divine. The divine is standing before all of us all of the time. It is the divine, and the divine alone, who appears in everything animate and inanimate. The divine is everywhere in the Universe. As holy rivers, high mountains, tender-hearted cows, sweet-voiced cuckoos, the upward-rising flames, the still stars—the divine pervades the whole creation in different forms. We should train our eyes to see the divine everywhere.

Nature is divine, sacred, and holy as well as abundant. All species are fed and nourished through the sacrificial act of life sustaining life. We humans are blessed with the gifts of nature. As long as we only take from nature what we need to meet our vital requirements, we are and we will be offered the gifts of food, water, and shelter. We must receive them with humility and gratitude and without abuse, waste, depletion, or pollution. As Mahatma Gandhi said, *"Nature provides enough for everybody's need but not enough for even one person's greed."* Waste is violence, pollution is violence, and accumulating possessions that are not essential to living is violence.

TREES

I think that I shall never see
A poem lovely as a tree.
A tree whose hungry mouth is pressed
Against the Earth's sweet flowing breast;
A tree that looks at God all day,
And lifts her leafy palms to pray;
A tree that may in summer wear
A nest of robins in her hair;
Upon whose bosom snow has lain
Who intimately lives with rain.
Poems are made by fools like me,
But only God can make a tree.

JOYCE KILMER

Nature is kind, compassionate, and generous; she is filled with unconditional love. From a tiny seed grows a great apple tree that produces thousands upon thousands of apples, year after year. The tree offers fruit without asking anyone for anything in return; it delights all comers with fragrant, sweet, nourishing fruit unconditionally. A saint or a sinner, a peasant or a philosopher, a human or an animal, a bird or a wasp, all are invited to enjoy fruit indiscriminately.

According to the principle of *yagna*, we should celebrate the beauty, the abundance, and the grandeur of nature by replenishing what we have taken. If we take five trees to build our home, we must replenish them by planting fifty trees. If we have taken crops of wheat, rice, and vegetables from the land and thus taken some goodness out of the soil, we must replenish the soil with manure and compost as well as leave the land fallow after seven years of cultivation. This is *yagna*: replenishment, restoration, and renewal. Vinoba Bhave writes: "If a hundred of us crowd together in one spot for a day, that will spoil the place and pollute the atmosphere, thus harming nature. We should do something to recoup nature, to restore its balance. It is for this purpose that the institution of yagna was created. Yagna is intended to reimburse, to put back what we have taken from nature . . . to make good the loss is one of the purposes of yagna." (From *Talks on the Gita*, Paramdham Prakashan Pavnar, Wardha, India.)

Nature seen as an inanimate machine becomes an object of exploitation, whereas nature seen as sacred becomes a source of inspiration for the arts, culture, architecture, and, of course, for religion and spirituality. We admire and pay tribute to great artists like Van Gogh for painting sunflowers, forgetting that sunflowers themselves are great works of divine art stimulating the imagination of the artist. If there were no sunflowers, there would be no Van Gogh; there would be no Monet without water lilies in the pond and no Cézanne without Mont Sainte-Victoire. Artists have always recognized the sacred quality of nature. Now it is imperative that scientists, industrialists, and politicians do the same and cease to think of nature as a mere resource for profit.

When we practice humility and gratitude, we are able to learn much *from* nature. But we in the anthropocentric, modern civilization learn *about* nature. There is a great deal of difference between learning "from" nature and learning "about" nature. When we learn "about" nature she becomes an object of study, leading to exploitation of her. That is why some scientists, such as Francis Bacon, have spoken about the human mission "to steal the secrets of nature." But when we learn "from" nature, we establish a close relationship with her. Then there is implicit humility and reverence toward the mystery of natural processes.

When we observe trees, we realize how everything is interconnected and interrelated. Photosynthesis allows the energy of the sun to feed the leaves of the tree, by the rain the tree is nourished, and soil holds the roots.

When we experience nature, we develop a deep sense of empathy and love for nature, and when any of us love something, we care for it, we conserve it, and we protect it. Much of the current environmental movement is driven by fear of doom and disaster. That cannot be the right motivation for a truly sustainable future. Love and reverence for the Earth will automatically result in sustainability, coherence, and harmony.

We need to realize that harmony is a fundamental principle of ecology. Wherever there is a breakdown in harmony there is discord and conflict. Our human responsibility is to restore and maintain harmony. The Iranian Sufi scholar Hossein Ghomshei says that the knowledge of universal harmony is science, the expression and communication of harmony is the arts, and the practice of harmony in our daily life is religion. Thus there is no conflict between science, the arts, and religion; they complement each other in pursuit of harmony. Many of our environmental problems arise because we have put the sciences, the arts, and religious practices into different compartments. If we wish to create a sustainable future and mitigate problems of resource depletion, population explosion, and the demise of biodiversity, then we need to create a coherence between science, art, and religion in order to live a life of harmony.

Care of the Soul

As we are urged by the Gita to live in harmony with the natural world, "soil," we are also guided to create harmony within ourselves.

Each and every one of us is a unique and special being. As the Sri Lankan art historian Ananda Coomaraswamy said, "An artist is not a special kind of person, but every person is a special kind of artist." He was talking about the immense potential of every human being.

In Sanskrit, the word for the individual soul is *atman*, the intimate being, and the word for the universal soul, or *anima mundi*, is *paramatman*, the ultimate being. Similarly, the Sanskrit word for the human individual is *nar,* and for the universal being (or God) it is *narayan.* In Arabic we find a similar formulation—the individual person is called *khud* and the divine being is called *Khuda*—just by adding an "a," the individual is released from his or her narrow identity or ego and transformed into divine consciousness.

The way to such an enlightened state is through self-knowledge, selfless service, and the surrender of the ego in favor of the understanding that "I am part of the whole." I am an organ of the Earth body; I am a member of the Earth community. As each branch is an integral part of a tree, every creature, human or non-human, is an integral organ of the Earth.

Often we are weighed down by the burden of our narrow identities of nationality, race, religion, class, gender, and similar other divisive concepts and mental constructs. We become imprisoned in the ideas of "I" separate from the "other" and "mine" separate from the "other's." Through universal love we are able to break out of this *ego* and become part of the *eco*—making a quantum leap by changing from "g" to "c".

The Greek word *eco* is very beautiful. From it we get "ecology" and "economy." Eco, or rather the Greek *oìkoς*, means home. In the wisdom of Greek philosophers, home is not only where we physically live—our house or apartment. The entire planet is our home, where 8.7 million species live as members of one household, one family; all species are kith and kin. Home ("eco") is a place of relationship, whereas "I" as a separate self or ego is a state of separation, disconnection, and isolation. Our soul gets starved in isolation. Therefore, let us return to our home. In our deep consciousness, let us reconnect with our Earth body.

When we realize "I am a microcosm of the macrocosm," we touch the mind of God, free from narrow identities, liberated from sorrow and separation, and free from fear and fragmentation.

Sometimes we become convinced that the world needs saving so urgently that we force ourselves to work day in and day out to save the planet. We join environmental or peace organizations. We go on protest marches. We work harder and harder for conservation of nature. As a consequence, we neglect our own well-being and suffer from burnout, depression, breakdown of marriage, and disillusionment.

The Gita teaches us that there is no need to separate caring for the soil from caring for the soul. We need to do both. The practice of the latter is called *tapas*, which means taking time for inner purity, meditation, spirituality, and living a life of elegant simplicity. Mahatma Gandhi said that we should be the change we want to see in the world. He believed there should be integrity between theory and practice, between word and action. Words gain power only when they are backed by a living example. This is why Mahatma Gandhi integrated time for prayer, meditation, solitude, study, gardening, cooking, and spinning into his day. He considered these activities as essential as campaigning for independence and working for the removal of untouchability. Thus, Mahatma Gandhi was an example of uniting the care of the external world with the care of the internal world. I will discuss the Gandhian approach in greater detail in Chapter Three, but here it is sufficient to say that the inner landscape of spirituality and the outer landscape of sustainability are intricately linked. We need to cultivate compassion, seek truth, appreciate beauty, and work for self-realization. Thus through meditation we can connect outer and inner ecologies. Meditation is a preventative medicine to avoid the sickness of the soul, and it is a curative medicine for the healing of the wounded soul.

The contemporary environmental movement, in the main, follows the path of empirical science, rational thinking, data collection, and external action. This is good as far as it goes, but it doesn't go far enough. We need to include care of the soul as a part of care of the planet.

Care of Society

Care of the soil and the soul needs to be extended to include care for society. In spite of unprecedented growth in the economy, science, technology, and world trade, almost a quarter of humanity is hungry and homeless, while a similar number is overfed and over-housed!

After the Second World War, President Truman of the USA, speaking at the UN (United Nations), declared that there are two worlds—the developed world and the undeveloped world. By the developed world he meant the world of industry, technology, free trade, and industrial farming, which was expected to lift the living standards of all people; the undeveloped world was the world of small-scale agriculture, rural life, local economy, and low consumption, condemned as a life of poverty. Thus the mission of mainstream economists and politicians became to industrialize the world, create economic globalization, and allow the free market to solve the problem of so-called "undevelopment."

WHOLE BODY PRAYER

May our legs be strong and steady
May our feet tread softly on the earth
May our stomach be small and soft
May our belly be full of fire
May our heart be large and loving
May our soul be simple and serene
May our mind be calm and clear
May our spirit be free of fear
May our mouth mint sweet words and kind kisses
May our eyes see beauty below, beauty above and beauty all around
May our ears hear words of praise and music of the cosmos
May our hands be generous in giving and grateful in receiving
May our arms find joy in embracing
May our body be a temple of love.

SATISH KUMAR

But despite nearly seventy years of relentless effort toward industrialization, the suffering of people in the so-called undeveloped countries has continued to increase. Even in China, India, and Brazil, where governments, industrialists, and business leaders sacrifice their cultures and traditions and destroy their natural capital in order to follow the path of modern materialism, industrialism, and economic growth, millions of citizens are still living below the poverty line. Even where living standards have risen and cars, computers, and highways have proliferated, general well-being, human happiness, social cohesion, and job satisfaction remain a distant dream. It is crystal clear that economic growth and GDP are not the same thing as human happiness.

> *We can no longer afford indifference to suffering outside our borders; nor can we consume the world's resources without regard to effect. For the world has changed, and we must change with it.*
>
> US PRESIDENT BARACK HUSSEIN OBAMA

This new religion of materialism has grown side by side with the growth of militarism. Total expenditure on nuclear and conventional weapons has quadrupled in recent years without any sign of an increase in security or peace. Violence in one form or another—legal wars waged by governments or illegal wars waged by so-called "terrorists"—continues to occupy many parts of the world without any resolution of national or international conflicts.

Humanity is not only at war against nature, it is at war against itself: the values of profit, power, control, and greed rule the minds of mainstream politicians and industrialists. Advertising seduces the majority of people, who dream of a lifestyle of consumerism, comfort, and extravagance.

This state of affairs is hardly conducive to a vision of harmony, coherence, and well-being. Therefore, a strong social movement is needed to establish justice, equality, liberty, and freedom, leading to the well-being of all. This cannot be done merely by social engineering or political maneuvering. It can only be done by a spiritual awakening and a new awareness of the benefits of mutual care and selfless service. The Gita calls it *dana*, which means sharing, generosity, giving before taking, and rising above narrow self-interest.

In a culture where self-interest is promoted as a paramount value, one would naturally ask, why should we give up our self-interest? The *Gita*'s answer is, as Vinoba says, "*Because we are already highly obliged to society. We were totally defenseless and weak when we were born. It is society that looked after us and brought us up, we should therefore serve it.*" (From *Talks on the Gita*, Paramdham Prakashan Pavar, Wardha, India)

We have inherited great architecture: the Pyramids, the Taj Mahal, great mosques and cathedrals. We are blessed with so much literature, poetry, music, and so many paintings. We are enriched by the great teachings of enlightened masters such as the Buddha, Muhammad, Jesus Christ, Lao Tzu, and others. We have been endowed with philosophy, science, and technology. The list of gifts we have received from our ancestors and our fellow human beings is endless. We are indebted to them. And now it is our turn to contribute to that culture and civilization and ensure that no child in our human family goes without food, no sick person is left unattended, and that no country or community is afflicted by war, exploitation, or torture. We may not achieve this goal tomorrow, but efforts toward the well-being of all must start today, and we must rise above the narrow confines of self-interest and work toward mutual interest.

But that vision of working for mutual interest is never easy. There are vested interests in society that prevent us from acting in mutual interest and push us toward self-interest. The strong exploit the weak; the rich keep down the poor; seekers of power subjugate the powerless. In such a situation the Gita advocates struggle and action.

Mahatma Gandhi was one of the most ardent followers of the Gita principles. He practiced nonviolence, truth, and compassion, yet fought a battle against colonization and for freedom.

Activists such as Martin Luther King, Nelson Mandela, Václav Havel, Mother Teresa, and Wangari Maathai are examples of people who acted in the spirit of the *Gita*, offering their lives as *dana* for the well-being of society as a whole. From these outstanding activists we can learn the lessons of activism for social justice and strive to establish a new moral order of human dignity.

So the way of the Gita is the way of a spiritual warrior, a peace warrior, and an eco-warrior—what the Gita calls a *karma yogi*: one who practices the yoga of action and is engaged constantly for the upliftment and well-being of the deprived and dispossessed but who acts without desiring the fruit of his or her own actions. The Gita says that as the tree does not eat its own fruit and the river does not drink its own water, the *karma yogi* or an activist should not seek any benefit of his or her own action. Rather, they should offer their action for the benefit of others. That is *dana*.

A Trinity of Peace

The trinity of the Gita is like the three legs of a stool: through *yagna* we replenish the soil, through *tapas* we replenish the soul, and through *dana* we replenish society. But they are not mutually exclusive. All of us need to engage in all three types of action simultaneously. In a nutshell, we need to live a spiritual way of life and engage in the protection of the Earth, enlightenment of the self, and restoration of social justice. The ancient trinity of the Gita is as relevant today as ever it was.

This trinity of a holistic, interconnected, and ideal view of life is *a view* rather than *the only view* of life. Any formulation of an idea in words has a limitation. No formulation can be final or the Truth!

When we have an intellectual conviction and we get some theory or belief about Truth in our head, we think, "Oh, I know what is the Truth because I have read a book about the Truth, called the Gita (or the Bible or the Koran or the Vedas or the writings of Marx or Adam Smith). I know the Truth, why doesn't the world follow it and accept the Truth that I know?"

So we get this feeling that we need to convert other people to "our" Truth. That is the beginning of the problem, the beginning of war and conflict. It is where the all-inclusive spiritual approach ends and narrow exclusivity begins. The

Truth we know from books, from our intellectual theories, or from our past beliefs is a truth we must renew and refresh. As we must cook our food every day—fresh, we must find and experience our truth every day—fresh. The basic ingredients of food may be the same—wheat, rice, vegetables; the basic texture of the truth also may be the same—love, compassion, peace. Yet we have to apply them in everyday situations in an open, receptive, and unprejudiced way. Nobody has a monopoly on a final, perfect truth. The moment that we begin to think "I know the Truth, you must follow me," we have fallen into the trap of thinking that we are right and others are wrong. There is no one truth, there are many truths.

Peace begins with positive thinking. We must make peace with nature, peace with ourselves, and peace with all people.

When we talk about peace, we must not have a narrow view of peace. I propose a multidimensional approach to peace, a trinity of peace related to the trinity of Soil, Soul, and Society. In India we always pronounce the word peace three times: *shanti*, *shanti*, *shanti*—peace, peace, peace. Why three times? Because peace has at least three dimensions: inner peace, social peace, and ecological peace—making peace with yourself, making peace with the world, and making peace with nature. I believe that without inner peace, no outer peace can be realized. If our society is full of people who have no negative thoughts, people who have achieved a degree of peace of mind and have a peaceful soul, then naturally they will not fear. But if we have not been able to combat our personal fears, then it is very easy for governments and military leaders to encourage fear of an external enemy. This is the situation at the moment—we are ruled by fear. Fear of our neighbors, fear of socialists, fear of capitalists, fear of whites, fear of Blacks, fear of Hindus, fear of Muslims, fear of Christians. We are all divided in different groups and fear somebody. No wonder we elect leaders who spend so much of the world's resources on weapons! It may not be easy to see the connection between personal peace and political peace, between inner peace and world peace, but these two aspects are totally interlinked.

I am not suggesting that we must not work for world peace until we have achieved inner peace. We must work on both levels simultaneously.

The need for peace is not just "over there." We cannot expect the politicians to change the world and give us peace. Peace will not come from the Houses of Parliament. The New World will not begin in Whitehall, or the White House, or the Kremlin. As long as we expect the world to change in our image, it will not change. The fears, the mistrust, the competitiveness, and the insecurity we see among political leaders are reflected in our lives, accumulating and becoming national fear, national mistrust, national disunity, and national insecurity and being expressed in big military expenditure and the arms race.

So unless we make peace with ourselves, we cannot achieve world peace; we cannot even begin to understand what peace means. Our concept of peace is very much one-dimensional. We think that if only presidents and prime ministers of the world could get together and negotiate peace, the world would be at peace. We may want to get rid of nuclear weapons and even other conventional armaments, but otherwise we want to go on as before. We don't want to face the fact that the arms race has its roots in our souls. Freedom from fear of every kind and realization of peace within is the first step toward a peaceful world. Peace is more than the absence of war; peace is a way of life.

> *Freedom from fear of every kind and realization of peace within is the first step toward a peaceful world.*
>
> SATISH KUMAR

Together with inner peace, we need to make peace with nature. Ecological peace is a prerequisite for world peace. The peace movement and the ecology movement have been working as if they were not related. But now the time has come when we must create strong links between "green" and "peace." Credit must be given to the only group that is emphasizing this link, Greenpeace. All ecological and peace groups should focus on "green" and "peace" together. War is always an ecological disaster. Therefore, no ecologically-minded person can afford to ignore the need for disarmament. And disarmament will not be achieved without stopping the race to control natural resources of the world. At the moment, we think it is our birthright to exploit nature, conquer nature, and squander the planet Earth. We can do what we like for our comfort, our living standards, and our convenience.

It seems as if we are at war with nature. We wage war against nature because of our greed for unlimited economic growth. To satisfy that greed we are in effect saying, for example, that we should find more and more oil as fast as we can so that we can run more cars and more airplanes. We should be able to save time on every journey. Never mind what happens to our children, our grandchildren, and our great-grandchildren. We don't care. We want short-term economic benefits for ourselves. The way we treat the soil, the Earth, the land, and the way we put animals in factory farms, the way we treat our rivers, air, water, seas, and mountains, and the way we cut down forests shows our contempt for nature. We have become totally self-centered.

If we wish to make peace with ourselves, with nature, and with people, we need to look at our relationship with our work. We have to start thinking about our day-to-day life. How we live. We have to think what kind of work we do. The most fundamental expression of being at peace with the self, with the world, and with nature is to engage in the right livelihood. How many people are really doing their work without harming and damaging the Earth? How many of us do our work with great joy, with a sense of fulfillment, and satisfaction of the soul? How many teachers get up in the morning and think "Oh, I am going to school to teach my students; it is a great joy to impart something of myself to my students"? How many doctors go to hospitals thinking "I am a healer and I enjoy giving myself to my patients"? How many of us are in love with our work, and how many of us do our jobs only because we have to pay our bills? We live to pay our bills—what a waste of human life! Teaching, farming, cooking, office work, making a chair or a shoe can be and should be a work of art, an act of devotion. Work is worship, but not the kind of work we do today.

This kind of creative work, which leads to inner and outer peace, is seldom possible in the present economic system, which is in effect the economics of war. In order to maintain economic self-interest, nations use military strength. It is believed that strong military power is needed to protect markets in Africa, or Asia, or South America. If we consume the amount of energy we are consuming and if our life is dependent on oil from the Middle East or gas from Russia and exports of cars and computers to Africa and Asia and imports of tea, tobacco, coffee, and clothing from everywhere in the world, of course we will need an army to give us access to natural resources. And we are not the only ones with our eyes on oil; the Chinese would like a large share in it too. So would the Indians. They can't accept that only the British, French, Germans, and Americans have the right to all the oil in the world.

Whether they are called communists or socialists or capitalists, all of them have created the economics of war. If those who want peace think we can get rid of war without changing the economic system, it is an illusion. We have to change the war economics of the present day into an economics of peace. Such economics will have much greater self-reliance, and trade, if any, will be based on fairness and not on exploitation. At the moment, the strongest in any economic power struggle gets the biggest benefit. When there is a bargain between the Indians and British, or Algerians and French, or Mexicans and Americans, the Americans and the Europeans dictate the terms of the trading because they are stronger. Even in the negotiations at the WTO (World Trade Organization), the Western nations get their way under the façade of fairness. They hold the levers of power in their hands.

The world we live in is a world governed by clever people. E. F. Schumacher used to say, "The world has become far too clever to survive." Policies are made by people who are paid big salaries, drive big cars, and own big houses, and these clever people are taking our planet to the brink of disaster. But when we speak about the unity of the world and peace on Earth, they say, "Oh, you are too naive. You are too idealistic. Your concept is simplistic. You have to face the real world."

Now the time has come for the idealists, the naive, the simple, to speak up. The time has come when the meek, who have no military or great industrial power behind them, can bring peace on Earth. We have had the industrial revolution. Now we have the internet revolution. We have conquered space. We have produced nuclear weapons. We have an explosion of consumerism. Yet all this is not enough. We are still obsessed with "economic growth." We are absolutely obsessed with materialism. All our energy, our thinking, and our research is going into it. The government's time and media time is devoted to promoting economic growth.

Industrialized countries need to rise above this obsession. We have enough. Unless we know when enough is enough, there will never be enough, because there is no limit set. But the moment we know when enough is enough, we will realize we already have enough! We need to share what we have more equitably. We need not spend all our time on economic matters. We can and should spend our time on building world peace, inner peace, and ecological peace. But when do we do it? We have no time. All our time has gone into our materialistic pursuits. Why are we so busy? Hundreds of years ago, when people had less economic growth, less material advancement, they had time to build magnificent churches and cathedrals in every town and city of Europe. How did they have the time and patience to build such things? Now we have no time, we want prefabricated buildings. Where has all the time gone?

The root cause of all our conflicts and peacelessness is in negative thinking. One side thinking negatively reinforces the other side's negative thinking, whether it is between Catholics and Protestants, between Jews and Palestinians, or between Americans and Russians. If there is any chance of peace being established, we have to begin with positive thinking. Protestants putting themselves in the shoes of Catholics, Jews putting themselves in the shoes of Palestinians, Americans putting themselves in the shoes of Russians, and vice versa. We must begin by being compassionate and positive, by putting ourselves in the shoes of others, and realizing we are members of one human family.

Here is a simple suggestion that might initiate a climate of positive thinking. Each day, preferably at the same time, give one minute to meditate and pray for peace. One minute is a very small contribution, but to remember it and do it every day is the most important thing. In India there is a concept of *mantra*, which means you use a word like a battery and charge it every day with spiritual energy by focusing on it. The following is the mantra of peace:

> *Lead me from Death to Life,*
> *from Falsehood to Truth,*
> *Lead me from Despair to Hope,*
> *from Fear to Trust,*
> *Lead me from Hate to Love,*
> *from War to Peace,*
> *Let Peace fill our Heart,*
> *our World, our Universe.*
> *Peace, Peace, Peace.*

Politicians, business leaders, even police and military personnel should say this prayer every day. If we meditate upon this mantra daily, it will act as a seed. Of course, it is not enough to put a seed in the garden and not attend to it, not nurture it. But unless we plant a seed, there is nothing to nurture. In the same way, if we use this mantra as our prayer for peace, it will give us a focus and allow us a moment of calm in which we can reflect on the state of our soul, the state of society, and the state of our soil, the environment.

If millions of people in the world start meditating upon this mantra and praying for peace, naturally there will be a change of climate, a change in minds and hearts. Peace will not come through presidential summits; it will come only when there is a change of atmosphere, a change of thinking, a change of attitude in the minds of people in the East and the West. If that happens, institutions will change, governments will change, economic and political systems will change, and people will take control of their lives and their local affairs. Thousands of actions will take place. A daily meditation for peace will act as a catalyst.

A minute a day is a good start. Then you may like to extend this practice to ten or twenty minutes. Such practice will help to train and transform your mind to be free of negative thoughts. Whether it is peace or war, praising or blaming, it all begins in our minds. If the mind is pure and positive, our words will be sweet and kind; and when our words are loving and positive, our actions will be caring and compassionate. Therefore, begin with your mind, look at the thought process going on within you. This is why meditation is so vital.

Meditation for Healing

Meditation is a method for the healing of the soul and bringing peace in the world. The words "meditation" and "medicine" are related to each other. They come from the Latin *mederi*, which means "to pay attention" and "to take care." When we pay attention to our physical body in order to take care, particularly at the time of some disease or unease, we take medicine. Similarly, when we pay attention to our inner being, our soul, spirit, and emotions, we undertake the practice of meditation.

When I teach meditation, I guide students through the following.

First of all, pay attention to your body posture. Sit comfortably, use a cushion if required. Relax your shoulders. Relax your arms. Relax the front and the back of the body. Relax your thighs, knees, and calves. Relax your feet. Feel the energy flowing through your spine upwards. Relax your neck. Relax your head, forehead, eyes, cheeks, chin, lips, tongue, and jaw. Relax your whole face. Relax your whole body. Let go of all tension.

Bring your palms, joined together, near to your heart and bow to the sacred universe, acknowledging that you are a microcosm of the macrocosm.

Then place your hands on your knees, resting palms upwards. Make a circle with the index finger and the thumb of both your hands. This circle represents the sun, the moon, and the Earth. Also, the circle is a symbol of the cycle of time and the cycle of life. The three remaining fingers stay straight, representing the past, the present, and the future simultaneously.

Pay attention to the silence, to stillness, and to calmness. Let your mind relax. Now all is well within you and around you in the world. Suspend your thoughts, worries, and plans. Smile at the world.

Let your mind focus on your breath. With the inbreath, say silently, "I am breathing in." With the outbreath, say silently, "I am breathing out." Follow the journey of your breath through your body, through the chest, through the abdomen, through the legs, and through the arms. Experience the breath nourishing your whole body.

Be aware of the beginning, the middle, and the end of your inbreath and your outbreath. Pay particular attention to the turning point from inbreath to outbreath and from outbreath to inbreath.

While you are breathing mindfully, be aware of each stage of your breath and be aware of the sensation of the breath within your body. Be aware that all human beings are sharing in the same breath of life that you breathe. Thus the whole of humanity is connected with you. Thus we are all related. With this sense of the unity of all life, bring your attention back to your breath; breathe gently and naturally.

As you breathe mindfully with full attention in a relaxed body, be aware that not only the whole of humanity but even plants, animals, rivers, and mountains are sustained by the same breath of life you are breathing. Thus we are all connected, we are all related. With this sense of the unity of all life, bring back your attention to your breath and smile.

There is a mantra in Sanskrit that is the seed of all mantras: OM. Repeat it three times, sing it to your own tune. Take a deep breath and chant the syllable, lengthening it as long as you can. Be aware that this sound is reaching to all corners of the universe and returning to you. Let this sound be the vehicle of compassion and wisdom. All living beings, not just humans, with whom you share your breath are your kith and kin, your friends. You have no reason to be in conflict. Let all your anxiety drop. Let your mind be calm. Breathe mindfully and smile. Let your fear dissolve. You belong to the Earth; be at home, all is well. Relax and breathe mindfully. The sun, the rain, and the soil will nourish you. Have trust. Breathe mindfully, take a deep breath, and smile.

Bring compassion to your heart and say, "May all beings be happy, may all beings be at ease, may all beings see good upon this Earth, and may no one suffer from fear, anxiety, or disease." Feel that your heart is full of love for everyone but particularly for those who may have lost their way. They need your compassion.

Resolve that in your life you will seek truth, love, and compassion. Resolve that you will seek beauty, unity, and generosity. Then offer your thoughts, words, and actions for the well-being of all, for now and for the future.

Breathe mindfully and smile. Be aware that your body is fully relaxed, enjoy these moments of calm, stillness, silence, and mindful breathing. Smile.

Say to yourself, "My intention is to think, speak, and act mindfully and attentively throughout the day." Then there is no distinction between meditation and living. Meditation is to pay attention to every moment of life, and therefore it is a way of life.

To conclude the meditation, bring your palms together, hold your joined palms against your forehead, and bow to the sacred universe and sacred life.

Then bring your joined palms near your heart and express your gratitude to life: gratitude for sunshine, rain, for the fertility of the soil, for the care you have received from your parents and other relations, gratitude to friends, gratitude to ancestors, gratitude to all. Gratitude to Soil, Soul, Society.

Feel a sense of joy, contentment, and fulfillment.

As you hold your palms together, imagine that all opposites complement and make whole: left and right, dark and light, above and below, masculine and feminine, negative and positive;

seeming opposites are two aspects of one whole. With this sense of wholeness, completeness, and interrelatedness, conclude this session of your meditation.

Sitting in such a session is helpful practice for the care of the soul—to learn to pay attention and take care of yourself and of all your relationships with others in an appropriate and harmonious manner. You can live a joyful life, free of fear, anxiety, and attachment. It is in your hands.

If every one of us pays attention in this way and lives calmly and joyfully, then naturally the world will be a better place, a beautiful place. If we be, do, and make everything mindfully and with attention, then inner and outer beauty will flow throughout our lives.

Beauty Imperative

Beauty is the food for soul. It is essential and not a luxury. Beauty is for everyone and not for the few. Being beautiful is more than being pretty. When something is in the right proportion, right balance, and right relationship, then we experience a sense of harmony, a sense of comfort and joy, a sense of ease and well-being. That is a beauty experience; it is more than outer appearance, more than a visual pleasure. Beauty is a blissful source of fulfillment.

We experience beauty with our whole being, through all senses and beyond. Beauty nourishes our bodies, minds, and souls. It heals our hearts and feeds our intellect. Beauty is an inner quality as much as an outer quality. Inner beauty and outer beauty are aspects of one single reality. Wholesome thoughts, good feelings, kind words, humility of hearts, and generosity of spirit help to create conditions in which we radiate beauty externally.

> *I walk in beauty before me*
> *I walk in beauty behind me*
> *I walk in beauty above me*
> *I walk in beauty below me*
> *I walk in beauty all around me*
> *The whole world is beautiful*
> *The whole world is beautiful*
> *The whole world is beautiful*
>
> BASED ON A NAVAJO SONG

Truth, beauty, and goodness are a continuum. When truth embodies beauty, goodness is born. There cannot be goodness without truth and beauty. Truth by itself is not enough; it is too sharp, too harsh, too blunt and must be adorned and imbibed by beauty. When we speak the truth, we should speak it beautifully and sweetly so that no one is hurt, no one is harmed. Beauty makes our words and actions enjoyable, tender, kind, and good. Sweet and beautiful words should also be truthful. Truth and beauty go together. Poet John Keats wrote, "Beauty is truth, truth beauty—that is all/ Ye know on earth, and all ye need to know."

William Morris advised us, "Have nothing in your houses that you do not know to be useful or believe to be beautiful." Thus, he was able to bridge the gap between the beautiful and the useful; there is no conflict between the two—they must live together. My mother went a step further; she used to say, "Whatever you make should be beautiful, useful, and durable at the same time. Just beautiful? Not enough. Just useful? Not enough. Just durable? Not enough. All three at once." I call it my mother's BUD principle.

The culture of mass production and consumption has sent beauty into exile. Modern, utilitarian architecture has brought about the uglification of our cities and towns. Prefabricated buildings, business parks, industrial estates, tall banks, high-rise apartments, superstores, and malls have all ignored the timeless qualities of proportion, balance, harmony, and human scale. This divorce between function and beauty is creating confusion, congestion, and conflict.

Beauty is a prerequisite for healthy homes, healthy cities, healthy society, healthy economy, and healthy life. Our architects and city planners need to bear beauty in mind while contemplating urban design. Parks and gardens, trees and ponds, flowers and fruits are not a luxury, not an add-on; they are essential ingredients for a healthy, happy, and harmonious city. Every home, every office, every shopping center, should be lined with avenues of trees, herbaceous borders, and flower beds. Good colors, good smell, good taste, and good touch bring good health and good luck. This is the beauty imperative. Nature and culture are identical twins. We separate them at our peril. In this separation, nature suffers and culture diminishes.

William Morris championed the movement for Arts and Crafts. He believed that when we build a house with our hands, make furniture in our workshops, make pots and paintings in our studios, plant fruits and flowers in our gardens, we transform ourselves into alchemists, turning ordinary into extraordinary. When we are creative, we become the creators of beauty. We discover our inner artist. We are all potential artists. When we transform ourselves from being a mere shopper and consumer to being a maker and a creator of beauty, we become artists.

Beauty leads to love: love of simple and elegant objects, love of home, of nature and of life, love of humanity. Love of beloved. The peacock dances to arouse love in our hearts, swans swim to stimulate tender feelings in our spines, a deer hides in the forest to provoke our curiosity. Beauty gives birth to love, and love gives birth to longing and romance. Beauty and love turn life into an occasion of rejoicing. Let beauty be the measure of humanity.

AS WE EMBRACE BEAUTY, WE ALSO NEED TO EMBRACE ETHICS AND MORALITY.

Moral Imperative

We all know and should know right from wrong. Honoring the integrity of our planet is as simple as doing the right thing. At the moment, the human mind seems to be totally preoccupied by the imperative of economic growth.

CARING FOR SOIL, FOR NATURE, FOR THE
ENVIRONMENT IS A MORAL IMPERATIVE.

The specter of debt, deficit, recession, and unemployment hovers over much of the Western world. Caring for and protecting nature is seen as a luxury for the good times. For the moment, concern for conservation care of soil is considered an impediment to economic growth. The environmental agenda has been pushed to the bottom. The priority for politicians, industrialists, and business leaders is to build more airports, more motorways, more high-speed railways, more office blocks, and more housing estates to stimulate economic growth. But you don't have to be a genius to see that there must be a limit to the number of airports, motorways, and business parks that can be built on the limited space of the British Isles or on the finite planet of ours.

What will we do when we have covered all our land with concrete, all our fields and farms with industrial parks and shopping centers, and when we have cleared all our forests to make way for those airports, motorways, and other urban developments or industrial farms? Sooner or later, we will reach our saturation point. Therefore, we need to think of an economic system that is durable and sustainable; a system that will provide livelihood and well-being for all people, not just for our lifetime, but forever.

This means that instead of a linear economy, we need a cyclical economy. If we base the economy on the health of forests, they can provide fruits, fibers, and timber forever. If we protect green fields, they will produce food until the end of time. If we harvest our energy from the sun, rain, and wind—instead of from dwindling fossil fuels—we will never run out of renewable power. If we use manual labor—the human hands—then our muscle power will remain inexhaustible. And of course, this cyclical, natural, and renewable economy must be built on a human scale with zero waste.

If truth be told, the world is not in economic crisis, and the land is still producing food. What we have is moral crisis. Humanity has lost its way. The answer is not more of the same old paradigm and more of the same industrial economy dependent on fossil fuels, but to move toward a natural, sustainable, and low-carbon economy. And with this perspective, the environment becomes an economic as well as a moral imperative. We, the present generation, have no right to take the forest, fields, and fisheries from future generations. It is morally wrong to deprive them of the security of natural resources.

No ethical standards would permit us to fill our oceans with plastics and our biosphere with carbon dioxide. It is the moral responsibility of every generation to leave the land in as good a shape—if not better—as when we inherited it from our ancestors.

This moral imperative goes even further than our responsibility to future generations. We have no moral right to impinge on the integrity of the biotic community. The human species is not the only species inhabiting the Earth. We must honor the rights of other species, who are members of the Earth community. Due to our expanding industrial economy and its emphasis on unlimited economic growth, we have been endangering the lives of millions of creatures. Diminishing biodiversity through industrial and economic activity is wrong on both economic and moral grounds. And it is as simple as that.

2

World in a Lotus

Just fearing pain, pain will not go away. Facing it, recognizing it, and accepting it, we can put pain in perspective, put it in its place. Pain is part of the universal scheme of things.

Buddha was a healer of soul. He taught everyone not to despair in pain. Pain is part of life. Only a living body can feel pain. Only a living heart can feel sorrow. Only through pain can you give and take birth. We all have to go through the pain of growing up. We all have to experience the aches and pains of old age. We all will experience the pain of death. Physical pain is often obvious, but we also go through psychological, emotional, and spiritual pains. Just fearing pain, pain will not go away. Facing it, recognizing it, and accepting it, we can put pain in perspective, put it in its place. Pain is part of the universal scheme of things. This is the first noble truth of existence.

Be it physical pain or psychological suffering, there is a cause of pain. Can you seek out the cause? Is it your unnatural living? Or inappropriate diet? Or unnecessary anxiety? Or undesirable anger, attachment, or illusion? What is it? Meditate upon the cause. Find it out. You cannot deal with your pain and suffering properly without knowing its cause. This is the second noble truth.

Do not despair. Suffering arises, suffering passes. What begins also ends. Have trust and confidence. You have the innate ability to deal with all your pain and suffering. Your intelligence, your creativity, and your ingenuity are dormant within you. Use the power of imagination and skillful means and you will be able to overcome all your pains and problems. You will be able to reach a state of equilibrium and enlightenment. By positive conviction and confidence, we can find solutions to all conflicts, be they personal, interpersonal, international, or inter-religious, and we can reach a state of harmony. By changing our internal attitude, we change the external circumstances and conditions. This is the third noble truth.

Such harmony cannot be achieved by mere wishful thinking. There are eight practical ways to achieve well-being and harmony. The first is holding a right view of oneself and the world—a view that is unprejudiced, unbiased, and unconditioned. We have always to ask ourselves, "Is this the right view? Am I motivated by my ego and self-interest, or am I motivated by truth?" If you ask this question honestly, you will get the honest answer from your own inner voice and from your own inner heart.

Secondly, right view must be followed by right thinking, thinking that does no harm to anyone, including yourself, other people, and all non-human species. Right and wrong could be understood simply in terms of violent or nonviolent. If it is violent, it is wrong; if it is nonviolent, it is right. This Buddhist formula is applicable in all circumstances. Nonviolence is the touchstone of rightness. Right thinking is to think well of others and put the well-being of others before one's own. In fact, the well-being of others and the well-being of oneself are one and the same thing. However, outwardly it may appear that there is a conflict between one's own interest and the interest of others; if we want to be free of psychological and emotional suffering, we need to put the interest of others first. That way, you have ended any conflict and you have put yourself in the service of others.

Thirdly, right thinking enables right speech. Of course, we should speak the truth, but we should speak it gently, sweetly, and nonviolently. If you sincerely wish to be free of suffering and pain, then do not use your speech to condemn others, to put others down. Words spoken in anger will boomerang; they will come back to haunt you. You are likely to get anger in return. Firstly, your harsh words and your anger will bring discomfort to yourself and discomfort to others and, secondly, your harsh words may give birth to more harsh words from the recipient. So do not expect to be free of pain while using wrong speech.

Have courage to live simply but live well and joyfully.

SATISH KUMAR

Fourthly, take right action. Before you act, think—is this action I am about to take necessary? Will this action lead to well-being? If the answer is yes, then that is right action. Your happiness is dependent on right action. Do not blame someone else for your suffering or pain if your actions are not upright. Be mindful of your action. Make sure your action leads to harmony, joy, and peace.

Fifthly, find right livelihood. Your purpose in life is not only to earn a living; your purpose is to make a life. Therefore, your work must be based on your vocation, your inner calling. Do not seek success in terms of fame or fortune but seek fulfillment. Instead of looking for a job or an employment, look for a livelihood. A job may bring you money, employment may pay your bills, but that will not make you happy. Do not complain about your unhappiness while stuck in a job you don't want to do. Have courage to live simply but live well and joyfully. Your desire to have more, to possess more, to own more, and to consume more is bound to cause pain and suffering. Therefore, the path to painless living goes through right livelihood.

Sixthly, you may be working very hard in your life, you may be very attentive, very committed, and diligent, but if your effort, commitment, and diligence are devoted to oil-mining, promoting unfair banking, developing genetically engineered seeds, or administering the production of useless or harmful goods, then all your diligence is no good. Diligence is a virtue only if it is practiced in the right context and toward the right end, the well-being of all.

Seventhly, just as your diligence has to be rightly applied, so too does mindfulness. It could be that you are mindfully shooting, hunting, buying, or selling, but while doing so you are damaging the environment, distressing animals, or depleting resources—then even such a lovely word as "mindfulness" is no longer lovely. Wrong mindfulness will not bring an end to your suffering, so at every step of your life ask yourself, "Is my mindful action bringing benefit or bringing harm?" If the answer is the latter, then just mindfulness is not enough, but if the answer is the former, then that is right mindfulness.

Eighth and last, like diligence and mindfulness, concentration can be right or wrong, beneficial or harmful. Therefore, we always have to ask the same question, again and again: "Am I concentrating on the right things or is my concentration leading to upset, annoyance, irritation, depression, and sorrow?" If your concentration is of the right kind, then it is no different from meditation, and with right concentration as your quality you can transform everyday activities into spiritual practice, be it walking, cooking, gardening, mending, building, writing, speaking, or umpteen other tasks; they will all become joyful and a source of happiness.

These eight meaningful practices can bring an end to suffering. The Buddha cannot give you happiness on a plate; only you can be the master of your destiny. Happiness is your birthright, but you have to claim it, and you have to take charge of it.

But you like to have wrong views or wrong thinking, you use wrong speech, take wrong action, work at wrong jobs, eat wrong food—and yet you want to be happy, you want no suffering and no pain. How?

With right view, right thinking, right speech, right action, right livelihood, right diligence, right mindfulness, and right concentration you can solve all your conflicts, all your unease, and achieve equilibrium.

Soil as Teacher

One morning the Buddha was sitting in meditation, cross-legged, with his hands in his lap, the right hand above the left hand.

"You teach equilibrium and compassion. From whom did you learn this wisdom?" asked a disciple.

The Buddha lifted his right hand and touched the soil. Without speaking for a while, he sat in that posture. The disciple observed the Buddha and his new posture, which became known as the "Bhoomisparsha mudra," meaning "Touch the Soil posture."

The disciple realized that the soil is the teacher of the Buddha. There is no one as patient, resilient, forgiving, and generous as the soil. The soil sustains, feeds, and shelters all life. Humans tread on it, plough it, dig it, and build on it, and yet the soil forgives. Humans put one seed into the soil and the soil multiplies it into ten thousand seeds and provides nourishment in return. We, the seekers of truth and liberation, need to learn from the soil the qualities of unconditional giving, expecting nothing in return.

The disciple also realized that the Buddha chose to sit under a tree for his meditation; while sitting under a tree he was enlightened. He was enlightened because he observed deeply that all phenomena of the living world, embodied by the tree, are impermanent and totally interconnected, and through that mutuality and reciprocity the world achieves its harmony. The sun feeds the tree, rain feeds the tree, soil feeds the tree, the tree feeds the birds. The tree returns nourishment to the soil by dropping its leaves; what an interconnected world! As the tree, so is everything else. Life maintains itself by constant receiving and giving. In nature there is no hoarding, possessing, or owning; everything is in constant flux and flow. That was the meaning of "Touch the Soil" posture.

There is no one as patient, resilient, forgiving, and generous as the soil.

SATISH KUMAR

Another day, the Buddha was sitting by a pond, disciples gathered around him, everybody sitting calmly and in silence, waiting to receive the teachings; but the Buddha picked a lotus flower from the pond and looked into the eyes of the monks. The monks looked into the eyes of the Buddha in return, but there was a kind of blankness in their eyes. The blankness was caused by bewilderment and wonder. The Buddha kept holding the lotus. Moments later, a disciple named Ananda smiled joyfully at the Buddha, who returned the smile with equal joy. The Buddha placed the flower in the pond, got up, and moved away without speaking a word.

The rest of the disciples looked at Ananda in amazement and asked him, "While we were looking at the Buddha and wondering why he was holding the lotus flower in his hand, you smiled so joyfully that the master was delighted and he blessed you with his smile, with a twinkle in his eye. Please, Ananda, tell us what went on between you two?"

Ananda replied, "When I saw the lotus in the hands of our enlightened master, the Buddha, I saw it as a lotus, nothing but a lotus, just a flower from the pond. Then after a while, upon meditation, I saw the sunshine in the flower, I saw water in the flower, I saw mud in the flower; no mud, no lotus. Then I saw the Buddha in the lotus; no lotus, no teaching of the Buddha. In that moment of great teaching, I saw the lotus and the Buddha as one. I saw the whole universe in the lotus, I understood the meaning of co-dependent arising—everything is made of everything else— life is one, holding many elements within it and manifesting in many forms, but each totally dependent on each other.

When I realized this truth, the unity of all life, I was filled with joy, so I smiled. I think the Buddha understood what I had experienced. So he smiled too."

The disciples heard him in stunned silence. They too got a glimpse of this big truth.

The Buddha's teachings spread far and wide, even though he only went as far as he could walk. He spoke few words and communicated through many gestures. More importantly, he made a great impact by his living example. Even though there were no means of communication other than word of mouth, thousands upon thousands of people came to hear him, learn from him, and follow his example. What he taught was pure truth from his heart and he taught it with profound compassion for all people, irrespective of their background.

Toward the end of his life, a disciple asked him, "It appears as if you have reached the evening of your life. I hope that you will reincarnate again and again as our great teacher."

The Buddha replied, "I do not wish to reincarnate as a teacher. I will reincarnate as Maitreya, as friend. Wherever there is a spirit of friendship, I will be present there. Teachers and disciples should be friends, parents and children should be friends, brothers and sisters, husbands, wives, and neighbors should be friends. Even humans and animals, birds and insects, rivers and forests should be friends; maintaining each other, supporting each other, and living in harmony."

Such teachings are so inspiring. No wonder that, even 2,600 years after he passed, we still find his teachings so uplifting. It is not the person of the Buddha, not the historical Buddha, but the living Buddha within my heart who inspires me. Nevertheless, the Buddha was one of the great teachers who taught the way of healing Soil, Soul, and Society.

Uniting Learning with Living

Another great teacher, a contemporary of the Buddha, Mahavira, the founder of Jainism as we know it today, taught compassion for all sentient beings, reverence for all life, and caring for Soil, Soul, and Society.

I was born into a Jain family and became a Jain monk at the age of nine. For me it proved to be like going to a school, but this school was very different from any other school. In this school there was no difference between learning and living. Education as a monk was not to pass exams and get a job; education was for the liberation of the soul.

Before I could learn about liberation I had to learn about bondage. I had to learn what I was seeking liberation from. My teacher was named Tulsi, and I called him Gurudev—which meant "the divine teacher." Gurudev was no ordinary teacher and, therefore, I was not to be an ordinary student, seeking knowledge for some ulterior motive. I was seeking knowledge to heal the soul.

My guru said, "Before you learn philosophy, languages, literature, or any other subject, you need to learn humility. Through humility you gain knowledge and then from knowledge you learn even more humility."

"What is humility?" I asked.

"Humility is to completely surrender your ego, your desire to acquire knowledge as an object. Humility is to make total commitment to what you are learning and to the teacher, who is a channel of your learning. Such commitment requires total dedication and concentration. It requires learning by heart and sharpening your memory."

These were big ideas, and I was a small boy of nine. I remember being bewildered, but the guru reassured me. "Just retain these words at the back of your mind; don't worry about them."

"What does it mean to unite learning with living?" I asked.

The guru told me a story from the great Indian epic, The Mahabharata. Yudhisthira was the eldest of five famous brothers called the Pandavas. Yudhisthira came to learn Sanskrit from a teacher. The teacher gave him three lines to remember by heart:

Satyam vad	*Speak the truth*
Dharmam char	*Follow the righteous path*
Krodham ma kuru	*Do not be angry*

"You have twenty-four hours to learn these three lines by heart," said the teacher.

The next morning Yudhisthira came to the teacher. "Have you learned the three lines I gave you yesterday?"

"Sir, I have learned two lines but not the third line. Would you give me one more day? I will do my best to learn," said Yudhisthira.

"You are a very dull boy, very lazy." There was a hint of anger in the words of the teacher. However, the teacher gave him another twenty-four hours to learn his lines.

Next day Yudhisthira entered the room of the teacher, shy and subdued. "What's the matter with you, Yudhisthira? Come forward. Have you learned your lines?"

"Sir, I am sorry. I am very slow. I am still trying to learn the third line," said Yudhisthira.

"What! You must be the stupidest pupil that I have ever had." Saying that, the teacher hit Yudhisthira on the head.

"Sir, Sir! I have learned. I have learned. The third line is "Krodham ma kuru"—do not be angry—I have learned it at last."

The teacher was puzzled. "What do you mean that you have learned? Minutes earlier you said that you have not learned and now you have. How did that happen?"

"Sir, in spite of your being angry with me, I was not angry, so I seem to have learned it!"

In this case the pupil was a good student, but the teacher wasn't a very good teacher, I thought to myself. But fortunately, my guru, Tulsi, was a true embodiment of the unity of theory and practice, and so Tulsi telling me the story of Yudhisthira pointed me in the right direction. Day after day I learned about the meaning of Dharma.

"If you know the meaning of Dharma, you know the meaning of life," said guru Tulsi.

I learned that Dharma means much more than anything that can be explained in words. Like Tao, what can be spoken of Dharma is not Dharma. I have to experience Dharma and feel it in my soul. But if I have to use words, I can say that Dharma is the true nature of all beings; Dharma is to live according to our true nature and be our true selves. I have to learn my true nature. Who am I? Why am I here? How should I be and live in such a manner that is true to my soul?

According to Jain teachings, I am not merely my body. I am an embodiment of my soul, my spirit. I am a physical as well as a non-physical being. It is easy to know the physical reality but more difficult to know the non-physical reality, the reality of the soul, the spirit—the *atman*.

One of the instinctive and existential principles is that all living beings wish to live; none wishes to be killed. Therefore, killing, destroying, or harming life is against Dharma, whereas caring for and conserving life with compassion is following Dharma. This first principle of Dharma is translated as nonviolence, or, in Jain terminology, *ahimsa*, non-harming: nonviolence to yourself, nonviolence to other people and nonviolence to all creatures—animals, plants, insects, oceans, all life forms.

Even though complete nonviolence is not attainable, the Jains try to minimize violence from moment to moment and increase compassion day by day, hour by hour, and moment by moment.

I was only nine or ten years old, yet every day my guru asked, "Is your compassion enlarging?" I did not have any answer, but my guru would say, "You have to learn to swim in the ocean of compassion. There is no limit to compassion."

At one stage I asked my guru, "Large fish eat small fish, large animals eat small animals. Therefore, it appears to me that violence is an integral part of nature. Total nonviolence is impossible."

"It is a good point. But animals commit violence mostly for their survival, rarely as an indulgence. But humans seem to have the capacity to indulge in violence, to develop guns and bombs, to dominate and to exploit, to cultivate cruelty and exercise control; these tendencies need to be curtailed," my guru said. "A bit of anger and a bit of selfishness are part of human nature, but so are compassion and kindness. We need to weed out the poisonous plants of anger and pride and cultivate the flowers of compassion and kindness in the field of our consciousness."

I was given a soft woolen broom and instructed to sweep the ground before sitting down in case any ant or other small creature might be damaged by me. I was taught to carry the broom with me and sweep the ground in front of me while walking, especially at night, to avoid treading on any insect.

All Jains are necessarily vegetarians, so one day I asked my guru, "You taught me that even flowers, vegetables, herbs, and grains have soul. This means that we have to take life for our food. This is not nonviolence."

Guru answered, "You are right. All vegetation, all plants are alive. But in our practice of nonviolence, we say that first of all we will not harm any creature that has five senses, such as humans and mammals. That would bring an end to wars and killing of mammals in all their forms. Then we extend our nonviolence to creatures with four senses, three senses, and two senses. In Jain biology, vegetation is considered to be one-sense-life, and for human survival we have to take life; we take it in its simplest form. This is called progressively minimizing violence."

The guru continued, "Human consciousness has evolved in such a way that we are capable of making such distinctions between creatures of one sense, two senses, three senses, four senses, and five senses, and we are capable of evolving our consciousness into a consciousness of compassion. This compassion to all sentient beings is the key to liberation from attachment to your own body at the expense of other bodies. Through compassion you are also liberated from the desire to control, to subjugate, and to exploit others for your own gratification."

Progressively minimizing violence and maximizing compassion means a life of self-restraint. If nonviolence and compassion is the first and foremost principle of Dharma, then self-restraint is the second principle.

"The path to liberation from fear, anger, and attachment goes through a life of restraint. In restraint there is contentment. Nonviolence necessitates restraint," said the guru.

I was instructed to have no more than one change of clothes, no more than one meal a day, and no more books than I could carry on my shoulders; the books I carried were mostly handwritten manuscripts of religious texts called *sutras*, containing the teachings of Mahavira. I was learning many of the sutras by heart. Whatever I had memorized during the day I would recite in the evening before going to bed (around 10 p.m.). I would wake up or be woken up at 4 a.m. to recite again the verses I had learned the previous day. If I did not remember any of them, I would go back to the manuscript and relearn. My guru always emphasized the importance of learning by heart.

Guru said, "Knowledge in your head is like money in your pocket. You can use it at any time. Your knowledge has to be part of you—not mere information in books. You can live your knowledge only if it is in your blood and bones, in your deep consciousness." Guru continued, "The word sutra has two meanings, a thread and a spiritual text. As a threaded needle is more difficult to lose and, if lost, easier to find, so, if your mind is threaded with sacred texts, the sutras, you will not get lost in the world of cravings, desires, and passions."

I learned ten thousand verses of Jain sutras by heart during the nine years of my life as a monk. I recited them regularly in the evening after sunset, in the hours of darkness, and again in the pre-dawn hours.

I was taught to practice restraint in acquiring and using material possessions, but there was no need for restraint in acquiring knowledge of the sutras and the practice of compassion.

"Why do we teach and practice restraint? Because unre-strained consumption is a result of greed," said the guru. "Greed leads to anxiety, fear of loss, and deprives others of the means of meeting their needs. Restraint is a prerequisite for justice. All humans are equal. In fact, all living beings are equal. Therefore, why should anyone wish to accumulate and possess more than their need? Through our wisdom and knowledge, we must distinguish between need and greed. Greed will also cause envy, resentment, and jealousy among those who are deprived of their fair share."

The third, equally important, principle of Dharma is care of the soul. Each and every one of us is the center of our own world. The world is how we are, and the world is how we see it. Therefore, working to develop, uncover, and recognize the qualities of our soul is essential for self-liberation. From age nine to eighteen I was not only taught to practice nonviolence to all living beings and self-restraint, but also to develop soul qualities by long and deep meditation, the practice of day-long silence once a week, fasting for a day a month, and standing in solitude and stillness in the wild.

The world is how we are and the world is how we see it.

SATISH KUMAR

"The world is made of individual humans, individual creatures, individual rivers, individual trees, and so on. Therefore, caring for each and every individual will result in caring for the world. You cannot care for others if you cannot care for yourself," said the guru. "You are your own light, and you are your own darkness. You are your own friend, and you are your own enemy. Liberate yourself, by yourself. Others will help you. I will help you, but our help will only be effective when you help yourself. Like somebody else eating will not nourish your body. You have to eat to nourish your body. In the same way, you have to act to nourish your own soul. The journey of the soul may not be easy. You may have to go through psychological and emotional upheavals, doubt and despondency, but stay with it, persist, endure; others have gone through such experiences, and we have learned from them that there is a state of liberation, a state of enlightenment when you attain equilibrium. In that state of liberation, you are able to treat pain and pleasure, gain and loss, negative and positive with equanimity. The purpose of your learning, of your living, and all other endeavors is to attain that state of equilibrium and harmony."

In those years I learned the way of Dharma; Dharma is to practice nonviolence for the well-being of the earth, practice restraint for the well-being of society, and nourish yourself for the well-being of the soul.

Finally, Gurudev Tulsi said: "The three principles I have taught you are not to be taken as dogma. Our philosophy is rooted in the concept of a multiplicity of truths. Ultimately the truth is fluid like water. The truth is invisible like air. Therefore, learn to live in ambiguity, embrace uncertainty, practice flexibility, keep an open mind. There is no fixed or rigid goal. Each and every one of us has to find our own liberation, which goes beyond description, definition, pre-scription, or rules. Liberation means that you need to liberate yourself from rigid ideas about liberation itself. Be mindful, be open, be aware, go beyond intellectual concepts. When you are free you may not even know that you are free."

These were the teachings I received in my early years; teachings of the Buddha and teachings of the Jains. I learned the unity of nature, spirit, and compassion; a continuum of Soil, Soul, and Society.

> *The thought manifests as the word;*
> *The word manifests as the deed;*
> *The deed develops into habit;*
> *And habit hardens into character.*
> *So watch the thought and its ways with care,*
> *And let it spring from love*
> *Born out of concern for all beings.*
>
> BUDDHA

3

Be the Change

Whatever kind of government we have, the role of it should be of simple, subtle, and invisible coordination. Like the thread in the necklace.

In the last chapter, I described two ancient traditions that helped me find my perspective on the trinity of Soil, Soul, and Society. In this chapter I write about Mahatma Gandhi, who embodied care for nature, spirit, and humanity.

Mahatma Gandhi played a very special role in my life. When I was a Jain monk, someone secretly passed me a copy of his autobiography. What impressed me most about that book was his argument that to practice spirituality you don't have to forsake the world and become a monk. The true practice of spirituality, he maintained, has to be in the world, in everyday life, in politics, in business, and in domestic life.

I also understood from Gandhi that it is the motivation behind your action that determines the quality of your action. If you are in politics for power, fame, or money, then it is a politics of pride and materialism; but if your politics is in the service of society, care of the Earth, or purification of soul, then that politics is spiritual, leading to self-liberation and the liberation of others. These teachings led me to leave the monastic order, which I describe in my book *No Destination*.

Since I wanted to learn more about the philosophy and practice of the Mahatma, the great soul, I decided to live in a Gandhian ashram in Bodh Gaya where the Buddha had been enlightened while sitting under a tree. At the ashram I read Gandhi's book *Sarvodaya*—the well-being of all. This was in 1956, and I was twenty years old. India was a newly emerging nation, having achieved her independence from the British in 1947. There was much debate about the direction of the country. Some advocated communism: the success of the Soviet Union and China was a beacon of inspiration for young and radical activists of India. Others were advocates of free enterprise, looking to the American model of capitalism and industrialism. Then there were the democratic socialists, who wanted a mixed economy, taking the best from the theories of Marx and Adam Smith.

But Mahatma Gandhi had a different world view. He saw the fallacy, the narrowness, and the utilitarian foundation upon which socialist, communist, and capitalist systems alike were built. In essence, there was not a great deal of difference between them. These systems wanted to exploit and subjugate nature for human benefit. Such systems cannot be called holistic. Under the title of *sarvodaya*, Mahatma Gandhi designed a system by which human beings would minimize their material needs and maximize their quality of life through spiritual, cultural, artistic, and human values.

The term *sarvodaya* is composed of *sarva* and *udaya*. *Sarva* means "all"—not only all human beings but all living beings—and *udaya* means "well-being." sarvodaya includes all life and excludes none. According to sarvodaya, animals, insects, plants, forests, mountains, and rivers as well as humans have intrinsic value. Humans have no more license to exploit nature than they have to exploit other humans. It is the duty of humans to receive the gifts of nature with gratitude and humility to meet their basic needs, and they should always replenish what they have taken. Mahatma Gandhi proclaimed that there is enough in the world for everybody's need but not enough even for one person's greed.

When Mahatma Gandhi was writing in the 1920s and 30s, the idea of environmentalism or ecology was hardly on anyone's agenda. Gandhi never called himself an environmentalist, yet his idea of sarvodaya expounded a need for respecting the earth, reverence for life, and recognition of our profound relationship with air, water, and soil.

As a former Jain monk, I immediately understood the profound meaning of nonviolence to nature. In most people's minds, the meaning of nonviolence was limited to respect for human life, avoidance of human conflict, and elimination of the possibilities of war; for Gandhi, nonviolence went much further and deeper. We have to be nonviolent to ourselves, nonviolent to other people, and nonviolent to nature. Mahatma Gandhi knew that there is no limit to our wants, desires, and greed. The finite Earth cannot satisfy the infinite greed of an ever-increasing population.

Restraint in the Gandhian view does not mean deprivation, starvation, or misery; restraint means knowing the appropriate measure and living within our limits—recognizing that other species also need space, food, forest, and water. Humans have no right to take the share of other beings. This is the principle that leads to a life of elegant simplicity.

Sarvodaya does not recognize the superiority of the human species over other species. Humans are to be respected, as should be the other species. For example, when we want fruit, a fruit-giving tree is important. When we want water, a river is important, but when we want to enjoy a play or poetry, then Shakespeare is the answer. When we want warmth, we want our home. Sarvodaya recognizes the appropriate functions of each thing and offers due respect to each.

When we want to sleep, a bed is of great value; but when we are hungry, the kitchen is the most important place to be. Similarly, there is no hierarchy of species in the philosophy of *sarvodaya*. In the universe we all have our place, we are made of each other, we are all related. But with the human species in a ruling position, we not only exploit nature but throw our waste and pollution into the atmosphere, causing global warming; into the ocean, causing sea pollution; and into the land, causing soil degradation and erosion. Only through ensuring the well-being of soil, air, and water can we ensure our own well-being.

It is interesting to note that Mahatma Gandhi and Albert Einstein shared similar ideals. In a letter to a rabbi, Einstein wrote: "A human being is a part of the whole, called by us 'Universe,' a part limited in time and space. He experiences himself, his thoughts, and his feelings as something separated from the rest—a kind of optical delusion of his consciousness. This delusion is a kind of prison for us, restricting us to our personal desires and to affection for a few persons nearest to us. Our task must be to free ourselves from this prison by widening our circle of compassion to embrace all living creatures and the whole nature in its beauty. Nobody is able to achieve this completely, but the striving for such achievement is in itself a part of the liberation, and a foundation for inner security." (As quoted in *Full Catastrophe Living* by Jon Kabat-Zinn.)

Einstein and Gandhi had great admiration for each other—no wonder that they did, given their views of the interconnectedness of all life.

If the well-being of all (sarvodaya) is the ideal for society, then *swaraj* (self-governance) is the political way to attain it. Mahatma Gandhi was neither a mere idealist nor an armchair philosopher. He was a practical man of action. An ideal was only good if it was possible to put it into practice.

Swaraj is also made of two words: *swa* and *raj*; *swa* means "self" and *raj* means "to shine." In other words, the shining of the self and the self that shines. According to the Indian scholar Makarand Paranjape, "You might actually say that *swaraj* is another word for enlightenment;" political independence then, is a version of self-governance.

Writing in the *Harijan*, a weekly newspaper edited by Gandhi, the Mahatma outlined his vision of a good society: "Life will not be a pyramid with the apex sustained by the bottom. It will be an oceanic circle whose center will be the individual always ready to perish for the village, the latter ready to perish for the circle of villages, till at last the whole becomes one life composed of individuals, never aggressive in their arrogance but ever humble, sharing the majesty of the oceanic circle of which they are integral units. Therefore, the outermost circumference will not wield power to crush the inner circle but will give strength to all within and derive its own strength from it."

Makarand Paranjape comments: "In Gandhi's model of oceanic circles, we have a way of relating to one another very different from the pyramidal or hierarchical order of most societies. In the latter, you have a few people on top ruling the rest. As you go higher, the number gets smaller, until at the very top you have only one person. In Gandhi's model, the individual is the center of the oceanic circle, continually expanding their self to include family, neighborhood, village, state, country, and so on. What is wonderful is that Gandhi allows each person to be the center of his or her cosmos but does not limit anyone to the confines of themselves. Each self has the capacity to expand outward, to reach out to others, to sacrifice themselves for their welfare. So the self in swaraj is not a limited but an expanding one—a potentially unlimited self which can stretch to embrace the whole cosmos." (From *Acts of Faith: Journeys to Sacred* India by Makarand Paranjape.)

Mahatma Gandhi took his model of self-governance from nature. As the Earth's systems are self-organizing, self-sustaining, self-maintaining, and self-governing, so should be human systems. Whatever kind of government we have, the role of it should be of simple, subtle, and invisible coordination. Like the thread in the necklace. We hardly notice the thread, but it is always there. Similarly, government is there but citizens are empowered to manage their own affairs largely at a local level. Thus the maximum power remains in the hands of human-scale communities, including maintenance of essential law and order, provision of health care and education, and organizations of trade and transport.

Swaraj is possible only when we embrace the ideal of small communities, small cities, and small nations. For Gandhi, India would have cultural unity but political diversity and decentralization. On the one hand, we all are world citizens, members of one human family; but on the other, we are firmly rooted in our local communities and in our place.

In order to establish swaraj (self-governance), we need moral education on a massive scale and we need to trust in people's innate goodness and ethical sense.

According to Indian tradition, every creature, human and other-than-human, is basically good. Like water and air, human souls are pure. Contamination and pollution are aberration and not the norm. Selfishness, greed, exploitation of the other, and pursuit of power over others have emerged out of social and economic conditions. If we can restore social and economic justice and value people for their good qualities of kindness, compassion, and generosity rather than for their wealth, power, and status, people will aspire to develop their own spiritual qualities instead of competing for material advantage.

The key to the success of self-governance (swaraj) is appropriate scale of organization. In smaller communities, everybody knows each other; therefore any problems, conflict, or difficulty can be spotted and remedied immediately. In large cities and large countries, there is a great degree of anonymity and secrecy and because of that, we need big organizations to address crime, conflict, and violence. We need ever-increasing numbers of police, courts, and prisons. Therefore, in order to achieve self-governance, we need to give more power to local communities and encourage more economic activity at a local level. Then the burden of governance on central government will be much lighter. Rules and regulations will be simple and maintained locally.

This is not an impossible dream. Small countries like Switzerland and Bhutan have a greater degree of self-governance than large countries like India or the USA. For most of history, indigenous communities were largely self-governing on a decentralized pattern of democracy. The idea of large-scale nation states is a relatively recent phenomenon. The Soviet Union used to be a monolithic centralized system but that eventually ended, to the advantage of smaller states. Power can be even further decentralized without any loss to essential services and the welfare of people. Centralization of power has two reasons. First, lack of trust in people—it is feared that local people cannot manage their own affairs—and second, people at the top of large governments can exercise greater control for their own advantage.

Gandhi's idea of self-governance disregards both these reasons. In self-governance, we have to trust people and their ability to manage themselves and their good sense of right and wrong. Even if they make mistakes, their mistakes will be no worse than the mistakes made by the heads of states presiding over large governments or CEOs of large corporations.

The economic crisis overwhelming Europe and the USA would not happen if political and economic power were rooted in local communities because they will be more self-reliant and spot the problem at an early stage. Even if they sometimes fail, the impact of their failure will be lighter and limited.

Self-governance (swaraj) is a principle of participation by people in their own political lives rather than control by others. Therefore, it is a way of self-determination, a forum of true democracy rather than plutocracy and bureaucracy as they are largely practiced in Europe, India, and the United States under the name of democracy. The centralized, large states have failed to solve most human problems. For example, poverty persists even in the United States, never mind in Africa, India, or China. A country like the USA, with such huge resources and enormous land mass, blessed with advanced science and technology, still suffers from crime, depression, illiteracy, homelessness, and drug addiction on a massive scale. What is the advantage of having such a centralized superpower that is incapable of caring for its own people?

> *In self-governance we have to trust people and their ability to manage themselves and their good sense of right and wrong.*

SATISH KUMAR

Not only is the problem of poverty and social deprivation unsolved, but the big states are a greater cause of conflicts. A country like Bhutan, Norway, or Costa Rica cannot afford to go to war in far-flung countries or to have nuclear weapons or to subjugate their neighbors. If we wish to eliminate or at least mitigate the problems of poverty, deprivation, and international conflicts, we need to listen to Gandhi and explore the possibility of reorganizing our nation states into human-scale self-governing units.

However, as the Canadian academic Anthony Parel comments in a recent book, "The *swaraj* that Mahatma Gandhi wanted required not only the political *swaraj* (self-rule) of the nation but also the spiritual self-rule or *swaraj* of the citizen." Parel writes, "Gandhi's *swaraj* included political and economic swaraj and aesthetic renewal as well. However, even this would not be enough to have complete swaraj. To have complete swaraj the citizen would need the enjoyment of spiritual swaraj—inward freedom—achieved through spiritual transformation." (From *Gandhi: "Hind Swaraj" and Other Writings* edited by Anthony Parel).

Thus *swaraj* means self-rule rather than rule over others. If politics, economics, and social organizations are built on the foundation of spiritual transformation, then politics and business would again become a form of public service and the split between political and spiritual would be healed.

Gandhi particularly emphasized the personal dimension of swaraj because, he argued, if one is not free, one cannot make other people free.

The idea of *swaraj* is not a fixed concept; it is an ever-evolving process, an ever-unfolding journey, and not a final destination. We need not fear that perfect swaraj is impossible, we need only endeavor to maximize self-rule and minimize rule over others or being ruled by others.

When one is mindful of personal responsibility and social justice, one is also aware of taking care of the natural environment upon which life depends. There is no separation between personal, social, and environmental swaraj.

The third concept developed by Gandhi is that of *swadeshi*, which means economics of place, again based on the principle of participation by every citizen in the economic activities of their community. *Swa* means self and *desh* means place. The term was coined during the movement for the independence of India. At that time, cotton was exported from India to England, turned into cloth in the English mills, and then brought back to India and sold at great profit. Thus the Indian cotton industry was ruined.

The economy dependent on long-distance import and export was an economy for profit and not for people. Therefore, Gandhi led the movement for swadeshi, boycotting not only goods made in England but also goods made far away in Indian cities such as in the factories of Mumbai, Chennai, or Kolkata. It was in this context that Gandhi reintroduced the spinning wheel, encouraging people to spin cotton and to get it woven locally, thus bringing livelihood, arts, crafts, and community coherence together.

Swadeshi gives birth to dignity of labor—makes people self-reliant, self-sufficient, and independent of large manufacturers, traders, and clever exploiters who desire to concentrate greater and greater profit in fewer and fewer hands. Swadeshi gives importance to human-scale technology and tools rather than large factories. If technology or a machine aids human hands and makes work light, then that technology is compatible with swadeshi; but if technology replaces human hands and makes the workers redundant, then that technology is incompatible with swadeshi.

Mahatma Gandhi believed that what can be made locally by hand with simple tools and technologies must be given protection—such as the production of food, clothes, shoes, furniture, furnishings, pots and pans, and houses. Large-scale, capital-intensive, sophisticated technology may only be used for things that cannot be made locally, by hand, and with simple tools. Technology should be in the service of people and not people in the service of technology. When technology and the economy become the master and people become the instruments serving the industrial machine, then work becomes soul-destroying, soil-damaging, and undermines the harmony of society.

Globalization is the antithesis of swadeshi. Globalization depends on extensive systems of transportation using excessive amounts of fossil fuels, resulting in massive carbon emissions causing climate change. A local economy is a guarantee for securing livelihoods in a sustainable manner with a smaller carbon footprint.

Spirituality is not simply sitting cross-legged with closed eyes chanting "peace, peace, peace" or going to church on Sunday singing sweet hymns or reading the Vedas, the Koran, the Bible, or other similar religious practices. Swadeshi transforms farming, gardening, spinning, weaving, and making things of daily use into an act of devotion and service. As Saint Benedict said, "Work is worship," but it is worship only when the maker is able to use imagination and creativity in the making. Work cannot be worship or spiritual practice when the maker is reduced to a mere unit of labor engaged in repetitive drudgery for some distant market, working only to earn money to pay the bills. The industrial, global, free-trade economy has destroyed meaningful work.

Local, decentralized, human-scale work based on workers' vocations is good for the soul and more likely to be good for society and the environment. Therefore, swadeshi is a prerequisite for care of Soil, Soul, and Society.

The philosophy of *sarvodaya* (the well-being of all), the politics of *swaraj* (self-rule and self-organization), and the economics of *swadeshi* (local self-reliance) offer a complete program, a holistic solution, for most of our contemporary problems such as rising unemployment, depletion of natural resources, the threat of climate change, international conflicts, global poverty, alienation, ill-health, and crime. These three Gandhian precepts provide possibilities for total participation by each and every individual in the affairs of their community. These precepts empower individuals, strengthen communities, simplify social systems, and create meaningful politics.

Capitalism instead of sarvodaya, centralized politics instead of swaraj, and global economy instead of swadeshi are leading the world toward dangerous environmental degradation, total disregard for spiritual values in the body politic, and complete confusion of purpose in social organizations, making all aspects of society suffer.

As socialists have Marx as their philosopher and capitalists have Adam Smith as their guide, Gandhi should be the mentor for the movement for sustainability working toward a just and peaceful future. Once Mahatma was asked, "Mr. Gandhi, what do you think of Western civilization?" Gandhi replied, "I think it would be a good idea." He replied thus because so-called Western civilization is built on violence, aggression, exploitation of nature and people, competition, and control. A society that can build and use nuclear weapons cannot be called civilized. A civilization that can put animals in factory farms and treat them in a cruel manner cannot be called civilized. A society that can devastate rainforests to produce more and more food and then waste a large part of it cannot be called civilized. A society that can tolerate one-third of its population being without food, shelter, education, or medicine cannot be called civilized. A society that can turn a blind eye on child labor and pay slave wages to workers in poor countries cannot be called civilized.

> *Follow the golden rule—do not do to others what you would not like to be done to you.*
>
> SATISH KUMAR

Behind the facade of democracy, human rights, free speech, and rule of law, Western institutions are built on principles of selfishness, greed, materialism, consumerism, and elitism—in one word, "violence." The future that the green and sustainability movement wants to build has to be founded on the principle of non-violence: nonviolence to nature, to oneself, and to all people; such non-violence has to be the paramount principle of politics, economics, education, business, international affairs, and every other human activity, without hypocrisy and without exception. "Western civilization" wants to keep nuclear weapons for itself but prevent proliferation. The West prefers one law for itself and another for the rest, believing that they can do what they like for their own security but no one else can. The underlying motto of Western civilization is "Do what we say and not what we do," which means copy our ways of trade, technology, and consumerism so that we can benefit from your markets. Seek our protection under various military treaties, but don't aspire to be self-reliant—either economically or militarily. Buy our weapons, but don't make your own!

According to Gandhi, looking from the perspective of a non-Western country, this is not civilization. Civilization has to be built on the basis of equality, mutual respect, common good, justice, and fairness; in one word, "nonviolence"—in thought, word, and deed.

There can be no better guiding principle for the green movement than the principle of nonviolence, which simply prescribes that whatever you do, make sure your action does no harm to soil or nature, to yourself—psychologically, emotionally, spiritually, or physically—or to other people— economically, politically, or culturally. Follow the golden rule—do not do to others what you would not like to be done to you.

We need to go further than the French Revolution, which proclaimed liberty, equality, and fraternity. We must aspire to follow the trinity of Soil, Soul, and Society within the over-arching context of nonviolence as expounded by Mahatma Gandhi. Without the overarching context of nonviolence, without the holistic trinity of Soil, Soul, and Society, we cannot have a civilized world.

If various organizations, NGOs, and groups as well as individuals working in the field of development and the environment wish to find common ground on which all our different passions, activities, programs, and projects can stand together, then nonviolence with the trinity of Soil, Soul, and Society provides that common ground. The Gandhian concepts and practices of well-being for all in self-organized, locally based, dynamic networks provide a detailed blueprint for action and transformation.

This transformation, according to Mahatma Gandhi, begins with yourself. Don't ask someone else to transform if you have not transformed yourself.

Once, a renowned politician, articulate speaker, prolific writer, and ardent campaigner, Dr. Lohiya, asked Gandhi, "To be blunt with you, you are not a great orator, not a charismatic personality, and yet tens of thousands of people follow you. When you make a call to action, large crowds turn out. People listen to you. When other great speakers and famous politicians with handsome bearing and charming personalities make a call for action, only a few turn out. What is the secret of your magic? People talk about the 'Gandhi touch.' What is it?"

Gandhi was taken aback. After a pause, he said, "I don't know! The only thing I can say is that I have not asked anyone to do anything that I have not done myself."

"That makes sense," said Dr Lohiya. "It's your integrity, not the argument, which has such power, such an impact."

"Dr Lohiya, we have to be the change we want to see in the world," Gandhi replied. Dr Lohiya smiled and nodded.

There are many stories of Gandhi changing himself before asking others to change. Once, a woman who was a good friend of Gandhi's came to see him. She brought her son along with her and sat down in front of Gandhi while he was busy spinning cotton with his spinning wheel, which was a daily practice for him. The woman caught Gandhi's eye. Gandhi smiled at her.

"Bapu." Often Gandhi was called by that name, which means father."

"Yes, my dear, what brings you here?" Gandhi asked.

"I have a request. My son is too fond of sweet things, particularly sugar. Sugar in milk, sugar in yogurt, sugar with rice. I keep telling him that so much sugar is not good for his teeth or for his health, but he never listens to me. He respects you. I think if you explain to him, he might listen."

Gandhi looked serious and stayed silent. The woman looked at him and wondered whether she should have troubled him for such a trivial matter! After a long pause, Gandhi replied, "Forgive me, my friend. Would you mind coming again after two weeks? Come with your son and I will talk to him then."

The woman was puzzled and sorry. Gandhi was busy with great issues of the nation. She should not have taken their friendship for granted. However, since Gandhi had asked her to come back in two weeks, she could not refuse his invitation, and so she returned.

Again Gandhi was in his hut. There was always a regular time, while he was spinning, for receiving visitors with no appointment.

Gandhi saw the woman sitting with her son, exactly two weeks later. Gandhi looked at the boy and said, "Do you see my teeth? Some have gone and others are going. I am sure you don't want your teeth to look like mine. Try eating sweet fruit, even very sweet fruit, in moderation, such as dates and raisins, but avoid pure sugar and cakes."

"Thank you, Bapu," said the woman, "but can I ask you a question? You could have given this advice to my son when I came to see you the first time. Why did you make us come again?"

Gandhi replied, "At that time I myself was taking a bit of raw sugar in my food. How could I ask your son to give up sugar without giving it up myself? So for the past two weeks I have avoided eating sugar. Now I feel justified to ask your son to give it up as well."

"Thank you, Bapu, and please forgive me for putting you to such trouble."

Gandhi leaned forward and asked, "Why do you keep sugar in your house? Do you eat sugar?"

"Bapu, I don't eat sugar, but I keep sugar for the guests, especially to put sugar in their tea. Then I have to make sweets for the festivals," the mother replied in defense.

"Children are unlikely to do what parents say; they are more likely to do what their parents do," Gandhi exclaimed. "I hope you will be an example for your son!" Gandhi concluded.

There is another story. Once Gandhi expressed a desire to his personal assistant, Mahadev, "I wish to learn Sanskrit because I wish to read the Bhagavad Gita in the original. I know that you studied Sanskrit, will you teach me?"

Teaching Sanskrit to Gandhi! Mahadev found it a daunting idea, but he was quick-witted. He said, "Vinoba is really a Sanskrit scholar and an expert exponent of the Bhagavad Gita. Why don't you ask him, Bapu?"

Gandhi turned to Vinoba, who was sitting nearby. "Would you be kind enough to spare some time to teach me Sanskrit through the medium of the Bhagavad Gita? Then my two wishes will be fulfilled simultaneously."

Vinoba was delighted to have the opportunity to teach Gandhi, but he knew how busy Gandhi was, so he said, "How will you find time? Will you make a regular slot in your day for this purpose so I can be sure of keeping myself free for that hour?"

"Yes, you are right. We have to have a regular session. How about after the evening prayer and before going to bed?"

Vinoba agreed to this proposal. He knew the Mahatma was very punctual and regular in attending morning and evening prayers. However busy Gandhi was, he would not miss two things: his prayers and his spinning.

The lessons began at the appointed time and went on with clockwork regularity. The first chapter of the Gita was completed, which was easy—only forty-seven verses setting the scene of the great dialogue between Lord Krishna and the warrior Arjuna. Then the second chapter also started well and was going smoothly and regularly until verse number fifty-six, when Arjuna asks Krishna, "You instruct me to be wise and to be steadfast, to be equanimous. Please, Krishna, what is the definition of wisdom? How should a wise person speak, sit, walk, and be?"

Krishna answers, "When such a person gives up all desires and attachment and when one is content within oneself and when that person's happiness does not depend on someone else, then such a person is in possession of steadfast wisdom."

This was a very profound verse for Gandhi. The lesson finished. Gandhi went to bed asking himself, "How can I be free of all desires and attachments? How can I be happy within myself? I must do everything to be a man of steadfast wisdom."

The next day, Vinoba arrived promptly for the lesson. "I won't have a lesson tonight," said Gandhi. The next day, the same statement. The statement was repeated for many days. Then Gandhi said, "Let us start our lessons again, I am ready."

Vinoba was somewhat mystified. He said, "We need to be regular; constant practice is essential for learning Sanskrit and the Gita."

"Vinoba, I have not stopped learning Sanskrit and the Gita, or missed the lessons because of laziness or busyness," Gandhi replied. "The verse number fifty-six of the second chapter asks us to be free of our attachments and desires and be contented within ourselves. I have been trying to put into practice these teachings of Krishna in my life. During the past month I have been partially successful. Now we can move forward. I wish to learn the Gita not merely to know it intellectually but to live its teachings."

My last story of Gandhi doing his best to be the change takes place while he was the guest of Jawaharlal Nehru in his palatial house in the city of Allahabad. Nehru became the first prime minister of India. In the 1940s, while Gandhi was leading the Congress Party in the Independence struggle, Nehru was his second-in-command. They met frequently. Often imprisoned, they were the champions of the struggle.

After spending the night in discussion, Gandhi went to bed feeling good about getting the wholehearted support of

Nehru for the principle of nonviolence as the means for the movement for the freedom of India. Even though the house of the Nehrus was aristocratically comfortable, there was no piped water. Therefore, next morning Nehru himself brought a jug full of water and a wash bowl for Gandhi. Nehru had a towel over his left arm, and with his right hand he poured water into the bowl while Gandhi rinsed his face and cleaned his teeth. Nehru knew Gandhi planned to depart that morning—there was no time to waste, so as he poured water he asked his guest, "Bapu, how are we going to convince the majority of Indians to follow the path of nonviolence?"

"Our example will be the best way to convince them."

"Sorry, Bapu," Nehru said suddenly and anxiously, "Will you wait for a minute while I get some more water?"

Gandhi looked perturbed. "Have I finished all that water?" he asked. "I should have concentrated on my washing and not been talking about all these big ideas. I should have finished my wash with one jug of water."

Nehru was astonished. He could not understand what Gandhi was getting at. "Bapu, don't worry about it. I know you come from Gujarat, a dry and desert land, where water is scarce. But here we have no shortage of water. Two great rivers meet here in our city of Allahabad, then there is even a third river, a mythical river, which keeps the water table high in our wells, so let me get you another jug of water. It will only take a minute!"

"Nehruji, you may have three rivers flowing through your city, but that gives me no right to waste water. My share is one jug a day only."

Nehru noticed tears in Gandhi's eyes, which surprised him, but he soon realized that Gandhi was truly a man of self-restraint. Gandhi allowed Nehru to bring half a jug of water as an exception so he could complete his wash. "I know you will think I am being faddish, but I believe that there is enough in the world for everybody's need but not for anybody's greed, not to mention anybody's waste. Water is so precious, water is life itself. Abundance of it does not give us license to waste. We were speaking about nonviolence; for me waste is violence."

These stories give us ample evidence to show that, for Gandhi, nonviolence was a way of life and not merely a tactic in the freedom struggle.

THE "SEVEN BLUNDERS"

Wealth without work
Pleasure without conscience
Knowledge without character
Commerce without morality
Science without humanity
Worship without sacrifice
Politics without principles

MAHATMA GANDHI

4

Truths from Tagore

As Tagore did not seek heaven, he also dismissed the idea of seeking God separate from the Earth. For him, divinity, deliverance, and salvation were to be found in the world, in the here and now.

Rabindranath Tagore was a contemporary of Gandhi. If Gandhi pursued poetry through politics, Tagore pursued politics through poetry. I was introduced to the writings of Tagore when I lived in a Gandhian community in Varanasi (Benares). There, my bedroom was opposite that of my Bengali colleague and friend Shishir, who was a fan, follower, and devotee of Tagore's poetry and music.

Shishir was always quoting Tagore, translating him for me into Hindi and putting Tagore's music on the gramophone. This captured my imagination, and so I went to a bookshop and bought three books: one of poetry, *Gitanjali* (Song Offerings), for which Tagore had been awarded the Nobel Prize; a novel, *Gora* (The Fair-skinned Boy); and a play, *Dakghar* (The Post Office), all in Hindi translation.

Until then I had only heard of Tagore and had read a poem here or a song there, although I did know the song "Okla Cholo Re" ("Walk alone, even if nobody follows you or listens to you, don't give up, keep going, keep moving, keep flowing"). We used to sing it every morning and evening at our prayer meeting because the song resonated with the sentiments of Gandhi, who often said that even if you are in a minority of one, truth is truth, and you should stand up for your convictions. Of course, everyone in India, including myself, knew our national anthem by heart—a song composed by Tagore in praise of the diverse and delightful landscapes of the Indian subcontinent.

Thus I was familiar with the stature and importance of Tagore but only superficially; Tagore wrote in Bengali, a language I did not know, and therefore I had no easy access to him in the original. It was thanks to Shishir that I began to pay proper attention to Tagore.

Once I had done so, I discovered Tagore was a poet of the spirit as much as a poet mesmerized by the mystery and beauty of nature, a poet in the tradition of the mystic poets Rumi and Kabir. However, he did not only dwell in the divinity of flowers, rivers, and seasons. He was as much an activist poet as a nature poet.

I saw him as an Earth activist, a spiritual activist, and a social activist. His poetry and plays, his songs and stories, his talks and teachings, his imagination and creativity were all underpinned by a vision to serve the Earth, lift the spirit, and transform society. Tagore celebrated the beauty, integrity, and generosity of life on Earth manifested in myriad forms.

The song in praise of his native land of Bengal later became the national anthem of Bangladesh.

> *I have become my own version of an optimist. If I can't make it through one door, I'll go through another door—or I'll make a door. Something terrific will come no matter how dark the present.*

SATISH KUMAR

Unconditional and unlimited love of land permeates his work, but it comes across most clearly in one of his longer poems, "Earth." One could say that this poem anticipated the modern movement of deep ecology and sustainability.

In "Earth," Tagore uses the power of language and imagination to its utmost effect. He sings with delight of the mystery and magic of the mountains, meadows, farms, forests, deserts, oceans, rivers, animals, seasons, and spirits.

At that time, when the world was suffering from the habit of valuing the Earth only in terms of her usefulness to humankind, Tagore maintained the intrinsic value of the Earth herself. It is human life that is utterly dependent on the gifts of the Earth, not vice versa. Therefore, he urged people to free themselves from arrogance and to live with humility and in harmony with the Earth. Tagore totally surrendered himself to Mother Earth and called himself a lap child seeking refuge in her:

> *Mother, hold me please*
> *within the firmest embrace of your arms*
> *Make me your own, one who belongs to your breast:*
> *that secret source from where the fountain rises—*
> *of your vast vitality and varied delights –*
> *do take me there. Don't keep me away.*

Where is "there"? "There" doesn't mean any other world or heaven. When Tagore imagines himself to be in heaven, he concludes that his beloved Earth is a better place to be:

> *And gods, goddesses, today I must*
> *say goodbye to heaven. Gladly have I spent*
> *many millennia in the kingdom of the gods*
> *as one of the immortals, and had hoped to see*
> *at this parting-hour a hint of tears*

on heaven's eyes. But heartless, void of grief,
indifferent, this happy celestial land
just looks on.
Stay laughing, heaven. Gods, keep drinking your nectar.
Heaven is indeed your very own place of bliss,
where we are aliens. Earth—she is no heaven,
but she is a motherland; that's why her eyes
stream with tears, if after a few days
anyone leaves her even for a few hours.
The humble, the meek, the most incompetent,
sinners and sick men—all she would hold tight
in an eager embrace, fastened to her soft breast,
such is the pleasure a mother gets from the touch
of her children's dusty bodies. So let there flow
nectar in heaven, and on earth let love,
forever mixed with pains and pleasures, stream,
keeping earth's heaven-spots ever green with tears.

As Tagore did not seek heaven, he also dismissed the idea of seeking God separate from the Earth. For him, divinity, deliverance, and salvation were to be found in the world, in the here and now. God and spirituality are in everyday life. There is no need to forsake the world to find God. It is not in renouncing the world but in embracing the world that we can discover God within, God between, and God all around. It is clear in his poem "Renunciation":

Said a man fed up with the world in the depth of night,
"I'll leave home tonight for the sake of the God I adore.
Who's it that keeps me ensnared with this house?"

"I," said God, but it didn't enter his ears.
Clasping their sleeping infant to her breast,
his wife lay happily asleep on her side of the bed.
"Who are you all, maya's masks?" he asked.
"They are myself," said God, but no one heard.
"Lord where are you?" said the man, leaving his bed.
"Right here," was the answer, but still the fellow was deaf.
The child cried in his sleep and clung to his mother.
"Return," said God, but the man didn't hear the order.
Then at last God sighed. "Alas," said He,
"where's my devotee going, leaving me?"

For Tagore, divinity is not in otherworldly quests, not to be found in ornate and extravagant temples and palaces, not in ego-driven achievements of wealth, power, consumerism, and materialism, but in a simple, elegant, and natural way of being. The ordinary is the most extraordinary and the meek the most marvelous. When we have lost the simple and ordinary, then we will know the value of them. Tagore says:

A stick under his arm, a pack on his head,
at dusk a villager goes home along the river.
If after a hundred centuries somehow —
by some magic—from the past's kingdom of death
this peasant could be resurrected, again made flesh,
with this stick under his arm and surprise in his eyes,
then would crowds besiege him on all sides,
everyone snatching every word from his lips.

His joys and sorrows, attachments and loves,
his neighbors, his own household,
his fields, cattle, methods of farming: all
they would take in greedily and still it wouldn't be enough.
His life-story, today so ordinary,
will, in those days, seem charged with poetry.

Of course, whatever happens in the future, the present social systems are exploitative and discriminatory, perpetuating poverty and deprivation. Observing the human predicament, Tagore extends himself from being an Earth activist to a social activist. In his book of poetry, *Gitanjali*, he was unequivocal in raising his powerful voice.

Tagore was a people's poet, and the poor in particular were always in his heart. While managing his family estate, Tagore came face to face with the plight of impoverished peasants, workers, and laborers. His ideals of justice and equality prompted him to establish a rural bank providing microcredit to his farm workers.

Being a poet and a landlord was a strange combination, but Tagore's father trusted his poet son and considered him to be a more suitable manager of the land than any other member of the family. Tagore took the responsibility seriously and used it to improve the status of land laborers and of agriculture. He himself worked on the land in order to show respect to farmers. Tagore instructed his son to study agriculture and famously collaborated with an English agronomist, Leonard Elmhirst. Together they established the Institute for Rural Reconstruction and called it Sriniketan, House of

Grace. Tagore believed that working on the land is dignified, meaningful, and satisfying.

The twenty-year-long relationship between the poet and the agronomist was a rare and profound collaboration. Their regular exchange of letters, numbering over one hundred, paints a vivid picture of Tagore's social activism and commitment to uplifting the poor. In the letters one can read the agony Tagore felt for the predicament of rural society. Like Mahatma Gandhi, Tagore believed India needed more than an end to the British Empire, she needed an end to caste discrimination and social injustice; she needed an agrarian revolution.

"Plato had no place for poets in his republic," Tagore wrote to Elmhirst in a letter dated March 31, 1922, "but I would like to offer myself to be the poet laureate of village India." Tagore continued, "The culture of the imagination is not altogether superfluous for the purpose of agriculture." He longed for the intimate touch of what he called "mother dust." He not only made a connection between imagination and agriculture, he also connected peace with agriculture. In the same letter he wrote: "Real peace comes from a wealth which is living, which has the blessings of nature's direct touch, which is not machine made—let us seek it humbly, coming down to the soil, dealing with the forces of life which are beautiful and bounteous."

Tagore was critical of city people who looked down on the rural population. On December 10, 1923, Tagore wrote to Elmhirst, calling him "the renowned champion of the village," and added, "while the city, proud of its fat purse, comes down to the village to extort sacrifice, must the village in its

turn prostrate itself humbly before the gate of its rich tor-
mentor for a pitiful morsel of favor? You ought to be able to
give to the world an emphatic 'no,' and hasten at once back
to the bosom of Bhoomi Lakshmi." *Bhoomi Lakshmi* is the
prosperous goddess of the Earth; use of this phrase shows his
profound reverence for the land. His commitment to rural life
was not merely for reasons of material development, but for
the development of the spirit, the imagination, healthy human
relationships, and the cohesion of human communities.

> *I slept and dreamed that life was joy. I awoke and saw that*
> *life was service. I acted and behold, service was joy.*

SATISH KUMAR

On June 26, 1924, Tagore wrote to Elmhirst, "Sriniketan
should not only have a shape, but also light so that it might
transcend its immediate limits of time, space, and special purpose." Economic development should "illuminate the path of
pilgrimage and not merely fill the storeroom of benefits" and,
furthermore, "a lighted lamp is the end for us and not a lump
of gold. We must avoid trying to do a particular kind of good
according to some recipe made by clever and learned men who
have technical knowledge and specialized experience. Let us
bring all our power of imagination and create a new world."

Tagore's ideals of rural development went beyond tech-
nology and science and more particularly beyond copying
Western models of economic growth. On October 21, 1926,
Tagore wrote to Elmhirst, "Europe has conquered the world

and now the time has come when she must conquer herself." What he intended was that Europe follow not merely efficiency but also seek to work with the living force of nature; therefore, Sriniketan should be a "center of life and not a mere school or college."

Science was very dear to Tagore's heart. He wrote a book called *Our Universe*, which was his scientific view of the world. He was in contact with scientists like Werner Heisenberg and Albert Einstein, yet he reminded Elmhirst that "Europe has got her science not as complementary to religion but as its substitute. Science is great, but it only affords us knowledge, power, efficiency—no ideal of unity, no aspiration for the perfect—it is non-human, impersonal, and therefore is like things that are inorganic: useful in many ways but useless as our food of life. If it is allowed to go on extending its sole dominion in the human world, then the living flesh of men will wither away, and his skeleton will reign supreme in the midst of his dead wealth." It is clear that in Tagore's view, science without spirituality or without humanity is dangerous!

Tagore was a public poet; his songs are sung by the people of Bengal irrespective of their caste, religion, or origin. His songs are for the Earth, for the spirit, and for humanity, but also his songs are often, implicitly or explicitly, of children and for children. He used the power of poetry to change the world. One of Tagore's greatest achievements was to establish what he referred to as a "Poet's School" at Shantiniketan, House of Peace. "The founding of my school had its origin in the longing for freedom," Tagore wrote. "But what is freedom?" In Tagore's words, "Perfect freedom lies in the perfect harmony of relationship, which we realize in this world—not through our response to it in knowing but in being." This being can be experienced and realized only by being embedded in nature. Tagore wrote, "Children can find their freedom in nature by being able to love it. For love is freedom: it gives us that fullness of existence, which saves us from paying with our soul for objects that are immensely cheap. Love lights up this world with its meaning and makes life feel that it has everywhere that enough which truly is its feast."

The objective of the poet's school was not merely the pursuit of knowledge but the pursuit of wisdom that arises when children experience nature. This is why Tagore insisted on holding his classes under trees. He is reported to have told his students that they had two teachers: "I am your human teacher, but these trees are your teachers too; learn the lesson of being from the trees." In his essay "A Poet's School," Tagore wrote, "A few coconut palms, growing by the boundary wall of our house, spoke to me of the eternal companionship which the greatest brotherhood of trees had ever offered to man. They made my heart wistful with the invitation of the forest." Tagore further wrote, "Seek freedom not in the man-made world, but in the depth of the universe, and offer reverence to the divinity inherent in fire, water, and trees, in everything moving and growing. The founding of my school had its origin in the memory of that longing for freedom."

This reverence for the universe's divinity and for "the brotherhood of trees" was so dear to Tagore that he abhorred the modern scientific idea of nature in tooth and claw. He said, "We find so often in Western literature a constant emphasis upon the malignant aspect of nature, in whom the people of the West seem to delight to discover an enemy for the sheer enjoyment of challenging her to fight."

Tagore's school provided plenty of opportunity for student's to obtain knowledge, but Tagore believed that "love and action are the only media through which perfect knowledge can be obtained, for the object of knowledge is not pedantry but wisdom."

Tagore was not interested in his students studying just to pass exams or merely to gain academic knowledge; Shantiniketan was an experiment in a holistic approach to learning. "I tried my best to develop in the children of my school the freshness of their feeling for nature and a sensitiveness of soul in their relationship with their human surroundings, with the help of literature, festive ceremonials, and also the religious teaching which enjoins us to come to the nearer presence of the world through the soul, thus to gain it more than can be measured—like gaining an instrument not merely by having it, but by producing music upon it. I prepared for my children a real homecoming into this world. Among other subjects learned in the open air under the shade of trees, they had music and picture-making, dramatic performances, activities that were the expressions of life."

Tagore pursued an education that takes account of the "organic wholeness of human individuality." Tagore explained, "Education is a permanent part of the adventure of life; it is not like a painful hospital treatment for curing a congenital malady of ignorance, but is a function of health and the natural expression of the mind's vitality."

The school practiced collaboration with nature and developed sensitiveness of the soul through constructive work. Tagore wrote that the students at his school "take the utmost delight in cooking, weaving, gardening, improving their surroundings, and rendering services to other boys, very often secretly, lest they should feel embarrassed."

> *He who wants to do good*
> *knocks at the gate; he who*
> *loves finds the gate open.*
>
> SATISH KUMAR

The educational activism of Tagore and the example of his school at Shantiniketan inspired Leonard Elmhirst to establish Dartington Hall school in England in the 1930s, and in the 1980s I, too, was inspired to establish The Small School in Hartland, Devon, where academic, physical, ecological, and spiritual dimensions are honored in equal measure. If children can have a taste of spiritual and physical freedom at an early age, they can build a world of freedom for themselves as well as for others in their later lives. Tagore's eco-activism, social activism, and educational activism are a beacon to enlighten our path of pilgrimage.

Tagore believed in the transformative power of poetry and the arts. He went beyond art for art's sake or art for self-expression, even beyond art for entertainment. He encouraged the idea of art for self-awakening and for the transformation of consciousness, for the enlightening of the soul, and, most of all, for changing the world. This thinking has inspired my editorial approach in *Resurgence* magazine, which now has merged with the *Ecologist*. Walking in the footsteps of Tagore, I have combined poetry with politics, ecology with economics, and invited the arts to permeate the magazine through beautiful images illustrating articles about renewable energy, agriculture, permaculture, science, social justice, philosophy, and religion—in other words, Soil, Soul, and Society.

THE GARDENER

Why did the lamp go out?
I shaded it with my cloak to save it
from the wind, that is why the lamp went out.
Why did the flower fade?
I pressed it to my heart with anxious
love, that is why the flower faded.
Why did the stream dry up?
I put a dam across it to have it for
my use, that is why the stream dried up.
Why did the harp string break?
I tried to force a note that was
beyond its power, that is why the harp string is broken.

SATISH KUMAR

And joy is everywhere; it is in the earth's green covering of
grass; in the blue serenity of the sky; in the reckless exuber-
ance of spring . . . in living; in the exercise of all our powers;

in the acquisition of knowledge; in fighting evils; in dying
for gains we never can share, joy is there everywhere . . . joy
is the realization of the truth of oneness, the oneness of our
soul with the world and of the world.

RABINDRANATH TAGORE

WALK ALONE, WALK ALONE

If no one comes at your call, then walk alone
Walk alone, walk alone, walk alone
If no one comes at your call, then walk alone
If no one speaks, unlucky as you are,
if no one speaks,
If everyone looks away,
if everyone fears
then open your heart,
find words for your thoughts
and speak alone
If no one comes at your call, then walk alone
If anyone, when the path gets tough,
loses the will to go on
Then bloody your feet with its thorns
and tramp alone
If no one comes at your call, then walk alone
If they offer no light, unlucky as you are,
If they offer no light
If in storm and rain and on dark nights
they shut their doors

then with the lightning
kindle a fire in your ribs
and blaze alone
kindle a fire in your ribs
and blaze alone
If no one comes at your call, then walk alone
Walk alone, walk alone, walk alone
If no one comes at your call, then walk alone

RABINDRANATH TAGORE

5

Head, Heart, and Hands

A forester does not need to put a tree in the seed; their work is to nurture the seed and help to bring the tree out of it.

One of the great inspirations I received from Tagore was his vision of holistic education that embraces universal values. I touched upon it in the last chapter. In this chapter I will explore and explain it further.

A few years back I was honored to be invited to speak at the London School of Economics or LSE. I was greeted by a professor. During the conversation I asked, "Do you have a department for teaching Ecology?"

"We do do some environmental studies, particularly in terms of business and sustainability, but we don't have a proper department for the study of Ecology," the professor answered.

"I am sure you know that economy means management of the household and ecology means knowledge of the household. How can one manage something one doesn't know?" I asked. Then jokingly I said, "The LSE is sending tens of thousands of graduates around the world for managing something which they don't know! No wonder the world's economy is a mess!"

"But our university was established for the study of economics and political science. Ecology is a rather new discipline that relates to the study of non-human species, whereas our university specializes in human institutions," the professor explained.

"In that case, perhaps you should think of changing the name of your university; perhaps you could call it LSEE: London School of Ecology and Economics."

The professor was amused. Our time was up. Students and lecturers had gathered in Hong Kong Hall to hear me.

I decided to explain to my audience that the name of LSE should be changed to LSEE because in my view the economy is completely dependent on ecology.

The Greek word *οἶκος* (pronounced *ekos*) means "home." In the wisdom of Greek philosophers, the home is where you live and where you have relationships. At home we have relationships with our parents, spouse, children, and so on, but our home and our relationships are not restricted to the place where we sleep, eat, and take care of our family.

In Greek philosophy, the idea of home extends further and further. Our neighborhood is also our home. So is our city, our nation, our continent, and the entire planet. All species upon this planet are related. We are made of each other, and we evolved together. The knowledge of these relationships, the knowledge that we are all interconnected and interdependent, is Ecology.

Unfortunately, most universities have reduced the meaning of the term "ecology" to the study of a particular species. But the study of a particular species is only a window onto the entire planet Earth and the understanding of our total interdependence.

Now economy has also been reduced to the study of finance, business transactions, trade, manufacturing, and consumption patterns. In the traditional, classic studies, students were taught three fundamental principles of economics: land, labor, and capital.

Land came first, as the primary part of economics. Land represented the entire natural systems and resources. Forests, rivers, stones, minerals, animals, and our relationship to them were all part of land management. Students were instructed to learn to use natural resources economically and take care of the land and all the gifts derived from it. But in modern economics, land has become a mere commodity, a mere means of making profit. The primary objective of agriculture is no longer to produce food to feed people. Agriculture has been turned into agribusiness. We have factory farms; we have monoculture; we have genetically engineered seeds. We have food prices controlled by market forces. We burn crops in order to maintain their market value. This is neither agriculture nor caring for the land.

The second principle of classical economics was labor, which meant people. Students were instructed to appreciate the importance of human skills, human ingenuity, human creativity, and human participation in a healthy economy. Young people were taught craftsmanship, and they were given profound experience of work in apprenticeships. Laborers proudly considered themselves members of the working class, and good business houses, such as Cadbury's and Rowntree's, ensured that their workers, their laborers, and their staff had good housing, good health care, and good schools for their children.

But in modern times workers have become mere instruments of making profit for business, and when they are no longer useful in profit making, they are made redundant or fired.

Of course, the third principle of economics, capital, is important, but it has the third place—capital has a place, but it must be kept in its place and not allowed to dominate the entire economic system.

In most universities of the world, business schools dominate. The study of land, of nature, and of the environment is given little importance and much less funding—it is considered some kind of idealistic and unrealistic pursuit.

In truth, the economy is a wholly owned subsidiary of the ecology. The reason we have an economic crisis is that we have an ecological crisis. We have been overconsuming our natural resources. We have been filling the atmosphere with carbon dioxide and other greenhouse gases in such quantities that climate stability is seriously threatened. Our oceans are overfished and plastic-filled. Our civilization is based on three words: waste, waste, and waste. Financial debt, unemployment, and poverty are all related to mismanagement of the environment. If we were to return to a state of harmony between ecology and economy and add ethics and equity to that combination, then we would have a better chance of creating a stable, steady, and sustainable future for humanity and for planet Earth.

By changing the name of LSE to LSEE, the university would be making a statement of embracing a bigger vision for the world than the present narrow vision of money management and business administration.

Most universities seem to have one object—getting their students to pass exams in order to get good jobs. Education is no longer about life, about practical skills, about development of imagination and creativity, but about earning money. We have brought the purpose of education to a very low level.

The meaning of the word "education" is to bring out what is already there, the potential of every student. Every soul has its own built-in intelligence. Knowledge and wisdom are intrinsic to soul. For example, every seed has its own built-in tree. A forester does not need to put a tree in the seed; his or her work is to nurture the seed and help to bring the tree out of it. In a similar manner, the work of a professor or a teacher is not to consider a student an empty bucket that needs to be filled with information. A teacher needs to observe the student, spot the potential, and help the student in such a manner that the dormant potential can emerge.

The study of ecology or of nature cannot happen by reading books, looking at films, or surfing the internet. To understand nature, we have to experience nature, we have to be in nature, and we have to learn *from* nature, rather than *about* nature. When we learn about nature, nature becomes an object of study. Much of scientific research has been to learn about nature so that we can exploit her. The scientist Francis Bacon studied nature in order to steal her secrets so that humans could control nature and use nature for profit; when we endeavor to learn from nature, we develop a sense of reverence for nature. Then nature is no longer an object.

The way to develop such a relationship with nature is to go out in the wild, in the outdoor classroom, and open your heart and mind to the mystery, magic, and majesty of the natural world. The present system of teaching is mostly within closed walls in modern buildings where classes are held under artificial light and with artificial air conditioning. I would like to suggest that universities and schools be built in open fields and forests rather than in the congested streets of an urban metropolis. Universities and schools should be surrounded by trees, ponds, and animals. Students should have the opportunity to roam, think, enjoy, and celebrate nature. All students and professors should have the opportunity, if they so wish, to grow food and flowers and manage orchards and forests in addition to their academic and theoretical studies. This is the way to be free of nature deficit disorder.

There is a growing movement for learning from the landscape in "forest schools" where children are offered time and the possibility to be in nature and play in the woods. But this is mostly limited to young children under the age of eleven. Occasionally and exceptionally, some schools for older children have short periods of outdoor activities. Our children know brand names and logos of multinational companies, but fewer and fewer children know oak from ash, wheat from barley, or bluebell from primrose.

The motto of our educational system has been to teach the "three Rs": reading, writing, and arithmetic. If you don't know how to read a label on your food packet, you are considered illiterate, but if you don't know anything about birds, trees, and flowers, about biodiversity, that is acceptable. You can have a BA, MA, or PhD despite being eco-illiterate, and you are okay. However, indigenous communities, peasants and farmers, bushmen and nomads—who have profound knowledge of forest medicine, animal behavior, and changing seasons—are considered to be illiterate savages because they cannot read or write. This notion of education through the "three Rs" has to be challenged. That is why we established The Small School in Hartland, Devon.

Go out in the wild . . . and open your heart and mind to the mystery, magic, and majesty of the natural world.
Education is about finding out who you are and becoming your true self.

SATISH KUMAR

When the school started, I said to the children, "Before we teach you Darwin and Shakespeare, learn to bake bread and grow cabbages and cucumbers. I have a profound respect for science and poetry, but they cannot and should not replace the knowledge of how to live. We all want to eat, but fewer and fewer people want to grow or cook food. We all want to live in a good home, but less and less people know how to build a house. We all want to earn money, but less and less people know how to respect and honor other people. Education has lost a sense of wholeness. Therefore, education should be about training head, heart, and hands, developing the power of thinking, feeling, and making. There is nothing wrong with the "three Rs," but they are not the whole story. Education is about finding out who you are and becoming your true self."

The modern system of schooling is all head, very little heart, and no hands at all. Politicians talk about preparing children for the knowledge economy and equipping them with information technology. They seem to believe that education should be of the brain and for the brain and by the brainy teachers. Schools aim to make children ready to compete in a world of banking, trading, administration, and management. Students coming out of schools and universities know nothing about making, growing, cooking, building, and manufacturing. Such manual activities are supposed to be performed by uneducated peasants and workers somewhere far away, in China or Vietnam or Indonesia or Morocco or some other distant land. This is a recipe for a disastrous future.

Because of our colonial past and because of our cleverness in managing money, we may have a high standard of life in the short term, but in the long term a stable society with happy people and a prosperous economy requires more than knowledge and information. It requires skills, craftsmanship, and a mentality that gives dignity to makers, growers, creators, builders, and workers. But our modern civilization has transformed people into mere shoppers and consumers.

In a well-balanced school or college, there should be properly equipped kitchens where students and teachers prepare their meals together. Healthy, delicious, and nutritious food is a prerequisite for a good community. Every school and college should be a community of students and teachers, not a knowledge factory. In order to liberate learning places from institutionalization, we should transform them into communities of learners.

Most school meals are manufactured on a mass scale and brought to schools ready-made. Often these tasteless meals are not eaten by students, and so a large percentage of food is discarded. Not that this food waste is turned into compost for the school gardens; rather, the food waste ends up in landfills, causing greenhouse gases. A large percentage of students in universities, who have to live in their own apartments, have not learned, either at home or in school, how to prepare proper meals, and so they eat cheap, processed, pre-prepared meals from supermarkets. No wonder we have to spend billions upon billions, year after year, on health care, and no wonder Western societies suffer from an increasing degree of obesity, cancer, and coronary diseases, not to mention mental, psychological, and emotional upheavals. Thanks to Jamie Oliver, there has been some awareness about the quality of food in schools, but educators are so obsessed with exam results and academic achievements that, for them, food and nutrition are extremely low priority.

The only thing school managements seem to care about is finding the cheapest and least troublesome source of school meals so that students can get on with their academic lessons, whereas students preparing meals should be considered an essential part of education.

Often school and university meals are served using throw-away plates and cutlery. Eating your meal with plastic spoons and from polystyrene plates is seen as a symbol of efficiency, economy, and progress. What a travesty of such concepts! School meals should be a time of community gathering and celebration of the fruits of the Earth. Instead, they have become a hurried affair. As you put petrol in the car, so you put pizza in your stomach!

In a good school, the kitchen should be considered a classroom where you learn many subjects without being taught. Therefore, when students are cooking, they are not missing their lessons. Cooking is, in itself, a great lesson. Students are learning to use their hands when handling vegetables, baking bread, and washing up utensils.

All schools are supposed to have playing fields, but very few have gardens to grow food, fruit, and flowers. It should be compulsory that every school has a garden, and as there are PE teachers, so there should be gardening teachers; as math and English lessons are compulsory, so should be the gardening lesson. Dirt is not dirty. We must give dignity to working with our hands, cultivating the soil. There are a great deal of health benefits from working outdoors in fresh air. Students are kept indoors for long periods under the present system, where they get bored, frustrated, and enervated. We need to revalue the importance of the outdoor classroom. Governments always organize and reorganize school structures, school administration, exam systems, and funding arrangements, but they never pay attention to some fundamental flaws of our out-of-date educational systems: children have little opportunity to be creative, to be makers, and to be growers. The garden is not only a provider of food, it is also a provider of knowledge and experience. In the indoor classrooms students get just information, perhaps a bit of knowledge, but very little experience; when they are in the garden, working with their hands, together with their fellow students and teachers, or in the kitchen, they get information, knowledge, and experience at the same time.

Why should we be compelled to put higher value on working in an office, or in a bank, or in a shop and a lower value on working in a kitchen or in a garden? No wonder there is increasing unemployment among the youth all over Europe.

Young people have not been taught any skills other than working in an office. And there are only a limited number of jobs in offices. Even if you have been trained as a doctor, a lawyer, a teacher, or a scientist, these are mostly intellectual occupations. I want education to include hand skills as well as head skills. The education system's exclusive emphasis on intellectual pursuits makes people dependent on goods produced far away. These goods have to be transported with enormous quantities of fossil fuels. When fossil fuels run out and people have lost the ability to make and manufacture, we will be extremely vulnerable.

In any case, using our hands and working with the soil has intrinsic value. Being self-reliant and participating in the process of life brings a sense of satisfaction essential for self-respect and psychological fulfillment.

When I refer to hand skills, I mean more than gardening. In my view, every school and every university should place equal importance on the skills of working with wood, clay, stone, wool, and other materials. Our educational system has given exclusive value to working with ideas, theories, and concepts. They are fine as far as they go—but without practice, theory is only in the head. In our daily life, we need to use our hands to make our lives worth living. Human energy is the most important source of renewable energy.

Environmentalists talk about renewable energy in terms of wind, water, and solar, hardly ever in terms of human energy. We have nearly eight billion people in the world. There is abundant human energy that is neglected, unused, and overlooked. If our schools and universities equipped our young people with the knowledge of using their muscle power to make and manufacture while using electricity sparingly, we would achieve greater sustainability. How wonderful it is to think that working with our hands not only keeps us healthy and happy, but also saves energy. As we are required to wean ourselves from dependence on fossil fuels to reverse the process of global warming and protect ourselves from the ever-decreasing supply of fossil fuels, we need to move toward an economy that is intimate, local, and ever-renewable. What is more renewable than human energy? And human energy comes from the food we eat. So first and foremost, human energy muse be used to grow our food in order to secure a limitless supply of human energy. Therefore, a garden in every school is not a fanciful idea, it is a sustainability imperative.

Now I turn to the education of the heart. What are the heart qualities? The answer is well-known. Learning to be respectful, grateful, compassionate, generous, and caring. Furthermore, learning to deal with your emotions, feelings, anxieties, and uncertainties. Our teachers have no time to engage with students to explore, to examine, and to reflect on the education of the heart. But how we deal with our feelings is just as important as English, math, history, and science. We know all about Darwin and Descartes, Milton and Marx, Shakespeare and Shelley, but we don't know how to respect each other, how to be compassionate toward those who are suffering from ill-health or misfortune, how to be grateful for the gifts of life that we receive every day, or how to care for the land, for animals, for forests and people.

The failure to engage with the heart qualities is dereliction of duty. We need nothing less than a revolution in education. We need to replace the "three Rs" with the "three Hs." This revolution is not too difficult; it only requires a change of heart. We will be striding toward a healthy society when we make our education truly comprehensive, inclusive, and holistic. By changing from the "three Rs" to the "three Hs" we would be moving toward the well-being of individuals, communities, nations, and planet Earth.

> *How wonderful it is to think that working with our hands*
> *not only keeps us healthy and happy, but also saves energy.*
>
> SATISH KUMAR

Emphasis on the "three Rs" has led to a competitive, self-seeking, and egotistical culture, whereas the "three Hs" will lead to a more cooperative, social, and ecological culture because the "three Hs" lead to relationships. Through our hearts we relate to other people and to nature. Through our hands also we relate to other people and to nature.

The Story of Satyakam

The education of head, heart, and hands was the fundamental principle of education practiced by Rabindranath Tagore. Learning *from* nature rather than *about* nature was his methodology. He held his classes under the trees, a practice which he inherited from the ancient Indian tradition, where learning took place in forest schools and in wild places, in nature and from nature.

One of the best-known stories is told in the Chandogya Upanishad.

A young boy, Satyakam, had heard of a great teacher called Rishi Gautama, who was a scholar and a sage. However, the Rishi accepted students only in small numbers and then gave full attention to the accepted student.

When Satyakam wanted to study under him, he was told that in the first interview the teacher would ask, "Who are you, what is your lineage, who are your mother and father, and why and what do you wish to study?"

Satyakam thought he was able to answer all these questions but one; he did not know who his father was. So Satyakam went to his mother and said, "There is a famous teacher in the forest. He is the only one under whom I wish to study, but he will want to know who my father is. So, Mother, can you tell me who caused my birth?"

His mother appeared embarrassed, a bit shy, but she wanted her son to study under a great teacher who would make Satyakam a wise and skillful man, so she replied, "My son, when I was a young woman, I was a servant girl. I worked for many men. Unfortunately and sadly, I do not know who caused your birth, but my name is Jabala, so go and tell your teacher that your name is Satyakam Jabala."

Equipped with this answer, Satyakam went to Rishi Gautama living in the forest, surrounded by sal trees, mango groves, and teak woods. The teacher lived by a lotus pond in a simple but elegant hut made of bamboo and thatched with straw upon which tender zucchinis grew.

Seeing Satyakam approaching, the teacher said, "Welcome, young man, what are you looking for?"

"I am looking for you, my master. I wish to learn from you and to serve you."

The teacher asked Satyakam to sit down on a straw mat by the pond and offered him cool water in a clay cup. "Will you be able to live in this forest, away from your mother and away from your friends?" asked the teacher.

"Yes, master. I long to learn from you," said Satyakam.

"Why are you so thirsty for knowledge?" asked the teacher.

"I want to find who is Brahman and who am I ."

"Who is your father? What is your lineage?" asked the teacher.

"When I asked my mother about my father, she said that when she was young, she worked for many men. Sadly, she does not know who my father is, but her name is Jabala and therefore she suggested that I let you know my name is Satyakam Jabala."

There was pure innocence in Satyakam's voice when he spoke. He was earnest and sincere.

"You speak the truth. Only a child of a good mother and a good father can be so truthful, and your desire for knowledge about Brahman is also pure and selfless. I take you as my student from this very moment."

Satyakam was filled with delight. He touched his teacher's feet with his head in gratitude.

"Go beyond that mango grove. There are nine cows and a bull there. Take them into the forest, care for them, and when these ten animals have become one hundred, come back. That is your first lesson."

Satyakam stood up and said, "I will do what you ask me to do."

The teacher blessed him.

Satyakam led the cows and the bull into the forest. First of all, he learned about gathering wild berries, fruit, and roots to feed himself. Within a few days he began to enjoy the taste, the fragrance, and the diversity of colors of such wild food. He realized the cows knew better than himself what to eat, what not to eat, when to eat, and when to sleep. Satyakam began to be friends with the deer and the monkeys, and he started to take deep interest in small, large, and colorful birds and to enjoy their singing. Satyakam lost all sense of time. He forgot his mother and his friends. The living creatures of the forest became his family. He made a flute from bamboo and started to imitate birdsongs, and when he played his flute cows stopped grazing and came to listen to his music. He walked in river valleys, over the hills and through a pathless landscape with cows as his companions. He lost all fear of the wild and season after season the number of his cows grew. Time passed quickly; he knew nothing of months and years; he only knew changing weather and changing landscapes. Thunder, lightning, and the time of the monsoon were the most exhilarating. After the monsoon fruit was in much abundance.

After a long time, a time without measure, he was standing under a teak tree playing his flute with all his cows and bulls gathered around him. Suddenly one of them said, "I am the hundredth member of the herd, newly born. Now is the time to return to our master. But before we start our return journey, I want to teach you about the existence of Brahman, the implicit and the explicit energy of the universe."

Satyakam was surprised! A cow teaching him about Brahman!

"Yes please, teach me who is Brahman, where is Brahman?"

The calf said, "The east is Brahman, the west is Brahman, the north is Brahman, the south is Brahman. Let us move on. Tomorrow, fire will teach us more about Brahman."

Satyakam was awed and exhilarated. He walked back with his herd of one hundred in the direction of his teacher.

The next day in the evening they camped on a hill. Satyakam gathered dry wood and built a small fire. As he was looking around at his herd, all healthy, strong, and relaxed, the goddess of fire emerged and said, "Satyakam, you have been a good forest dweller. As my gift to you, I will tell you a secret about Brahman."

Satyakam was once again surprised, but with full attention he said to the goddess of fire, Agni, "Please tell me who is Brahman; where is Brahman?"

"Animals are Brahman, birds are Brahman, insects are Brahman. Brahman is all around you. Tomorrow a swan will teach you more about Brahman."

Satyakam was full of joy to learn such knowledge about Brahman. He slept calmly and deeply that night; so did his herd. Next day they travelled through the forest, over the hills, along the river valley, and arrived at a lake. The sky was red, like someone had been painting the clouds. There were colors and light rarely seen. Satyakam was looking at the sky in a total trance. Slowly, slowly, the red sky began to fade, and clouds began to darken. Satyakam stood there until only a faint glow of light was present over the lake. In that light Satyakam saw a swan swimming closer to him, like a white jewel in the black night. Satyakam looked into the eye of the swan. The swan said, "Satyakam, I wish to reveal a truth to you, a truth about Brahman."

This time Satyakam was not so surprised. He smiled at the swan and said, "Please tell me who is Brahman, where is Brahman?"

"This lake is Brahman, this river is Brahman, this sunset is Brahman, these clouds are Brahman, this light is Brahman, this darkness is Brahman, these trees are Brahman, these hills are Brahman. Satyakam, tomorrow you will meet your guru. He will teach you more about Brahman. Let me wish you good night. Sleep well, dear pilgrim." Then suddenly the swan disappeared in the darkness.

Satyakam felt light and free. What a truth coming from the mouth of a swan! He lay down on the bare earth, his arm as his pillow, dreaming about Brahman and dreaming about the swan. Was the swan Brahman or a messenger? In his dream state the answer came—the message is Brahman, the messenger is Brahman. There is no message without the messenger; there is no messenger without the message.

Next morning the cows led the way and Satyakam followed. He heard the birds singing, "We are Brahman, they are Brahman, all are Brahman." A breeze was whispering into the ears of Satyakam, "Brahman before you, Brahman behind you, Brahman above you, Brahman below you, Brahman all around you. Keep walking, keep flowing into Brahman."

The sage heard the sound of the hooves of a hundred cows. He heard the flute of an accomplished player. He saw the dust rising above the mango grove. Then he realized that Satyakam was returning. He reached out for his walking stick and walked to greet his dutiful disciple. The herd was within sight and behind them was Satyakam. When he saw his guru, he ran and fell at the feet of the master. Suddenly the herd stopped. The teacher embraced Satyakam and said, "All the cows are healthy and strong. You too are healthy and strong. Your eyes are bright, your face is serene, you look wise and well."

"With your grace and blessings, I have become at home in the forest. These cows have been my companions. The birds in the sky and deer in the woods have been my brothers and sisters, I have been learning the secret and the truth about Brahman, first from the calf, then from fire, and then from the swan. But the deepest knowledge is still beyond me, so I am happy to return to you. Please teach me about the mystery of Brahman. Who is Brahman? Where is Brahman?"

The sage held Satyakam's hand and they walked toward the master's hut by the lotus pond.

"Satyakam, your eyes are shining. It is Brahman shining in your eyes. Your heart is full of love. It is Brahman who is your heart. The calf told you the truth. So did the fire and the swan. Brahman is within you and outside you. Truth is Brahman, love is Brahman, and beauty is Brahman. Breath itself is Brahman. The million names of a million things are nothing but the names of Brahman."

Rishi Gautama continued, "The universe is the dance of Lord Shiva—another name for Brahman. There is no separation between the dance and the dancer. And so there is no separation between the creator and the creation. Everything and everyone is a creator, and everything and everyone is a creation. Creation is continuous. There is no beginning; there is no end. Birth is Brahman and death is Brahman. Through birth and death life is refreshed and rejuvenated. Pain is Brahman and joy is also Brahman. Pain and joy make us strong and resilient."

Satyakam was blessed with deep understanding; his desire for knowledge was fulfilled. His head, heart, and hands were in total harmony.

6

Small Is Still Beautiful

*If economic activities are conducted at a small and local level,
then it follows that the human footprint on Earth will also be small.*

So far, I have written about how the wisdom of the East relates to the trinity of Soil, Soul, Society. In this chapter I write about a Western economist who was a philosopher and a man of faith. I met E. F. Schumacher in 1968 and found in him the embodiment of holistic thinking. He spelled out in some detail how human society could be at ease with itself, take care of nature, and still enjoy the fruits of constant spiritual renewal.

E. F. Schumacher was a champion of the green economy. He advocated smallness because it was compatible with greatness and greenness. Giant factories engaged in mass production and giant corporations engaged in mass consumption and mass transportation lead to the pollution of land, air, and water, the depletion of resources, and the destruction of human creativity. That is why Schumacher came to the conclusion that small is not only beautiful, it is also essential, even if it is not sufficient. Small is necessary because it provides the potential for people to be spontaneous, creative, flexible, and innovative.

At a smaller scale, we are much better disposed to exercise a greater degree of autonomy and to improve existing plans and rules according to changing circumstances. Moreover, we are better able to care for the natural environment, for ourselves, and for our human communities—in other words, Soil, Soul, and Society.

In 1962, Rachel Carson presented a scientific case for a greater understanding of and care for the natural environment in her book *Silent Spring*.

In 1972, the UN organized its first environmental conference in Stockholm, attended by many heads of state and government leaders, where a strong political case was made for a change of policy in favor of environmental protection.

At that time, the Club of Rome had published its seminal research under the title *Limits to Growth*, which made a strong plea for shifting the focus from consumption to conservation.

All this was very encouraging.

But E. F. Schumacher felt that unless we challenge the "religion of economics," the science and politics of environment was not enough. The world was gripped by a system of economics that was anti-people, anti-nature, and, moreover, soul-destroying. Schumacher had written a number of essays laying the foundation of an ecological and spiritual economics. Inspired by the work of Rachel Carson, the UN conference in Stockholm, and *Limits to Growth*, he set out to weave those essays together into a book. The result was *Small Is Beautiful*.

> *Small is necessary because it provides the potential for people to be spontaneous, creative, flexible, and innovative.*
>
> SATISH KUMAR

But from the beginning, the book was not easy. When Schumacher searched to find a publisher for the book, it proved an uphill task. Publisher after publisher sent him a "no thank you" note. In the end, a small publisher, Anthony Blond, spotted the potential of the book, originally titled *Homecomers: Economics as if People Matter*.

Having read the manuscript, Blond said to Schumacher, "What you are really talking about is that smallness is a prerequisite for human happiness and well-being, for social cohesion and environmental caring, for peace and for freedom."

Schumacher replied, "Yes, you are right, I am saying that, but I am saying much more than that!"

Blond suggested, "Why not call your book *Small Is Beautiful* and make "A Study of Economics as if People Matter" the subtitle? The title of the book needs to be snappy, short, and memorable."

Schumacher liked the idea; for him, beauty was as important as smallness. Small by itself is no guarantee of goodness. Small also has to be beautiful and good.

Therefore, getting these two words and concepts in one title with simplicity and accessibility was an attractive proposition. Schumacher said to Blond, "I like it. As you are the publisher, if you think your title will sell the book, then I am happy to agree."

Blond was pleased and published the book in hardcover in 1973. Just as Schumacher had difficulty in finding a publisher, so Blond had difficulty in marketing the book. The British media as well as the market found the book too idealistic and utopian. However, Blond was successful in getting the book published in the United States, where the media and academia resonated with it. Schumacher went on a book tour the length and breadth of the USA and spoke to packed audiences in universities, churches, and town halls. Jerry Brown, then Governor of California, got hold of a copy, read it, and was so inspired that he invited Schumacher to the governor's house. Talking to Schumacher personally was even more stimulating and impressive, so much so that Brown phoned President Jimmy Carter and insisted that the president meet him. Schumacher being invited to the White House became big news in the UK, and suddenly the media, MPs, academics, and booksellers in his homeland discovered him—the book became a bestseller. Soon it was translated into the major languages of the world, and today it is a green classic. The salient points of this groundbreaking book are as follows.

Organizations are conceived and built for some ideals, such as caring for the health of people, providing education for the young, producing and distributing food for people, or caring for the environment. Large-scale organizations tend to get bogged down in the maintenance of the organization itself, and the ideals for which an organization was set up tend to become secondary. Large scale often forces people to be at the service of the organization, whereas small scale tends to make the organization at the service of people.

One of the primary tests of an organization is whether it turns people into instruments to perpetuate the system and sees people as a means to an end, or whether the organization exists as a means with people as the end. Large business organizations aim to maximize profit—people become subservient to the profit motive, whereas smaller business organizations are better able to maintain a balance between the well-being of their members and the community they serve while keeping an eye on the bottom line.

Similarly, large government organizations become obsessed with their hold on power. Other human, social, and ecological considerations become subsidiary to the overriding imperative of remaining in control, even if lip service is paid to improving public services or maintaining sustainable development.

E. F. Schumacher wrote, "There always appears to be a need for at least two things simultaneously . . . freedom and order. We need the freedom of lots and lots of small autonomous units and at the same time the orderliness of large scale . . . when it comes to action, we need small units because action is a highly personal affair and one cannot be in touch with more than a very limited number of persons at any one time."

While Schumacher and other decentralist thinkers advocated the paramount importance of human scale, this was mainly a matter of physical organizations and not any kind of parochial, narrow, or nationalist confinement. Schumacher himself agreed that "When it comes to the world of ideas, principles, or ethics, to the indivisibility of peace and ecology, we need to recognize the unity of human kind."

Without any doubt we are members of the Earth community, and all national, political, religious, and industrial boundaries are of secondary importance. We need to recognize the sacredness and intrinsic value of all life without confining ourselves to any sectional or sectarian interest. But we are limited by our physical stature and therefore able to form active and personal relationships with only a few people. The whole Earth is our home, and yet we develop a sense of place and a spiritual connection with the place where we actually live. Smallness is not to be confused with narrowness. The idea of small was not a matter of dogmatic belief for Schumacher. He often spoke of appropriate scale. He highlighted the importance of smallness because he found the world obsessed with "an almost universal idolatry of giantism;" therefore, he found it necessary to insist on the virtues of smallness. "If there were a prevailing idolatry of smallness," Schumacher wrote, "one would have to try and exercise influence in the opposite direction." Schumacher further explained that "for every activity there is a certain appropriate scale."

Scale of Human Settlements

Not only political, social, and business organizations need to be built at an appropriate scale; human settlements must be planned on the principle of human scale. The mindless growth of cities around the world worried Schumacher enormously. "Millions of people start moving about, deserting the rural areas and the smaller towns to follow the city lights, to go to the big city, causing a pathological growth." Schumacher was concerned about the creation of megalopolises where tens of millions of people converge, creating congestion, pollution, and alienation while losing community, beauty, and simplicity.

> *The whole earth is our home and yet we develop a sense of place and a spiritual connection with the place where we actually live.*
>
> SATISH KUMAR

For Schumacher, the upper limit of a desirable city was about half a million inhabitants. In such a small city, citizens can walk from one end to the other without needing to get in a car or a bus. A citizen can access the school, shops, library, theatre, clinic, and other amenities on foot. There is a better balance between city and country; nature and culture live side by side. Such a city should be surrounded by farms, fields, and orchards to supply the city's needs with minimum transportation. Energy should be derived from sun, wind, water, and wood. Even a little bit of fossil fuel goes a long way if frugality and a no-waste policy are an integral part of city culture. Allotments, roof gardens, and water harvesting can all be possible in the city when people live together within the context of mutuality, cooperation, and care.

Schumacher explained: "The all-pervading disease of the modern world is the total imbalance between city and countryside, an imbalance in terms of wealth, power, culture, attraction, and hope. The former has become over-extended, and the latter has atrophied. The city has become the universal magnet, while rural life has lost its savor. Yet it remains an unalterable truth that, just as a sound mind depends on a sound body, so the health of cities depends on the health of rural areas. Cities, with all their wealth, are merely secondary producers, while primary production, the precondition of all economic life, takes place in the countryside. The prevailing lack of balance, based on the age-old exploitation of countryman and raw material producer, threatens all countries throughout the world, the rich even more than the poor. To restore a proper balance between city and rural life is perhaps the greatest task in front of modern man. It is not simply a matter of raising agricultural yields so as to avoid world hunger. There is no answer to the evils of mass unemployment and mass migration into cities unless the whole level of rural life can be raised, and this requires the development of an agro-industrial culture so that each district, each community, can offer a colorful variety of occupations to its members."

Economy of Scale

Small scale naturally leads to a local economy; large scale leads to globalization. Globalization is wholly dependent on excessive and wasteful use of fossil fuel, requiring massive infrastructure and mindless mobility as well as causing climate change. By contrast, local economy enhances a sense of place, a sense of community, and a sense of responsibility to the local environment.

Once, Schumacher noticed a lorry full of biscuits coming from Edinburgh to London, and a little later he learned that lorries carry biscuits from London to Edinburgh. As an economist, he failed to see why able and creative human beings are compelled to drive lorries for hours on end, going from Edinburgh to London and from London to Edinburgh, carrying biscuits at huge cost to the environment. Surely the Scottish recipes for biscuits could be learned by London bakers and vice versa, avoiding air pollution, human boredom, and road construction. After much thought and analysis, Schumacher could not work out the economic logic of this transaction, so he consoled himself jokingly, "Oh well, I am a mere economist and not a nutritionist, perhaps by transporting biscuits over long distances the nutritional content of the biscuits is increased!"

Not only biscuits but even water is transported long distances. I have seen Scottish Highland Water being sold in a French supermarket and French water in Scotland. I wondered why Scottish water is not good enough for the Scots and French water for the French. Of course, when there is trade between Scottish whisky and French cognac one can see the logic; that is proper trade. But what is the point of exporting and importing water?

Britain exports almost an equal amount of butter as she imports. The same is true with many other products. Schumacher was one of the first to point out the senselessness and stupidity of such a system.

In the name of the economy of scale we ignore the diseconomies of scale. While millions of people in Europe and the United States have no work and are forced to live on social benefits, goods are imported from China that could easily be made locally, providing work, reducing pollution, and liberating these countries from the enormous burden of debt.

Psychology of Scale

Small scale is also conducive to personal, psychological, and emotional well-being; the well-being of soul. In large-scale organizations, the integrity of the individual is often lost. The individual feels "nothing more than a small cog in a vast machine when human relationships of daily working life become increasingly dehumanized," wrote Schumacher.

Large-scale organizations are more concerned with efficiency and productivity, and the place of human happiness and spiritual fulfillment does not figure. Schumacher further explained, "Nobody really likes large-scale organizations; nobody likes to take orders from a superior who takes orders from another superior. Even if the rules devised by bureaucracy are humane, nobody likes to be ruled by rules, that is to say, by people whose answer to every complaint is, 'I did not make the rules; I am merely applying them.'"

People in large organizations do like orderliness, but that orderliness is often static and lifeless, and individuals within these organizations often lack a sense of adventure and the courage to take risks. Schumacher believed that the ideal organization is one where there is "plenty of elbow room and scope for breaking through the established order to do the things never done before, never anticipated by the guardians of orderliness." Schumacher cherished creativity, where an "unpredicted and unpredictable outcome" is encouraged.

Schumacher saw that "the specific danger inherent in large-scale organization was its natural bias and tendency in favor of order at the expense of creative freedom . . . the man of order is typically the accountant and the administrator; while the man of creative freedom is the entrepreneur. Order requires intelligence and is conducive to efficiency; while freedom calls for, and opens the door to, intuition and leads to innovation . . . without the magnanimity of disorder venturing into the unknown and incalculable, without the risk and the gamble, the creative imagination rushing in where bureaucratic angels fear to tread—without this, life is a mockery and a disgrace."

Ecology of Scale

If economic activities are conducted at a small and local level, then it follows that the human footprint on the Earth will also be small. Large-scale mass production gives rise to large-scale mass consumption leading to large-scale waste and pollution, whereas small-scale, local, and mindful production by the masses will result in careful consumption, incorporating the ideals of reduce, reuse, repair, and recycle into the objects and goods of daily use.

Schumacher's concern for smallness was not small for its own sake; he believed that small is sustainable and environmentally friendly. Modern society committed to a large-scale capitalist system looks at nature merely as a resource for maximizing profit.

> *In classical economics, the true wealth was land, forests, animals, minerals, rivers, human ingenuity, creativity, and skills.*

SATISH KUMAR

Land, labor, and capital, the principles of classical economics, have been turned upside down by modern economics. Capital has become the domineering master. In this model, land and labor exist to serve capital. In classical economics, the true wealth was land, forests, animals, minerals, rivers, human ingenuity, creativity, and skills. Financial capital was there to oil the wheels. In modern economics, money has become the wealth—whereas money should be considered merely a measure of wealth, a means of exchange, and not wealth itself. This primacy of money in the modern economic model is the cause of the environmental crisis.

The mission of the modern economy is to maximize profit and the method is to conquer nature. Industrialists talk of a battle with nature—they treat nature as if they were at war with her. Factory farming, genetic engineering, industrialization of ploughing and harvesting, the use of fertilizers, pesticides, and herbicides, clear-cutting of forests, opencast mining, deep drilling or fracking in search of oil, industrial fishing, and umpteen other examples are evidence of the fact that the industrial economy sees nature to be fought and defeated. The captains of the modern economy are unaware of the fact that if they win the war, they will find themselves on the losing side.

Schumacher considered nature to be the true capital, defining the word in its broadest meaning. He insisted that we should do everything we can to conserve, safeguard, and protect natural capital for her own sake and for the sake of future generations. Schumacher referred to respect and reverence for the intrinsic value of sacred nature as "meta economics." He wrote, "Fossil fuels are merely a part of the natural capital which we steadfastly insist on treating as expendable, as if it were income. If we squander our fossil fuels, we threaten civilization; but if we squander the capital represented by living nature around us, we threaten life itself."

If we were faithful to classical economics, then we would consume the gifts of nature with moderation and for the satisfaction of our vital needs.

The industrial and capitalist economy recklessly squanders natural capital "as if it were something we had made ourselves and could easily replace out of our much vaunted and rapidly rising productivity."

In Schumacherian economics, the aim is to create "health, beauty, and permanence and learn to live peacefully, not only with our fellow humans but also with nature." In capitalist economics the aim is to pursue continuous and unlimited economic growth, which Schumacher called pathological and which he considered to be an impossibility—one cannot have unlimited or infinite growth on a finite Earth.

Spirituality and Scale

The single-minded pursuit of economic growth is pure materialism in which greed is systematically cultivated and restraint, frugality, and wisdom have no place. According to Schumacher, we have become far too clever "to be able to survive without wisdom . . . the exclusion of wisdom from economics was something which we could perhaps get away with for a little while, as long as we were relatively unsuccessful; but now that we have become very successful, the problem of spiritual and moral truth moves into the central position."

Schumacher again and again highlighted the essential connection between economics and wisdom. He wrote, "The cultivation and expansion of needs is the antithesis of wisdom, it is also the antithesis of freedom and peace. Every increase of needs tends to increase one's dependence on outside forces over which we cannot have control, and therefore increases existential fear. Only by a reduction of needs can one promote a genuine reduction in those tensions which are the ultimate causes of strife and war."

Large-scale economics is the economics of war and violence. "Ever bigger machines, entailing ever bigger concentrations of economic power and exerting ever greater violence against the environment, do not represent progress: they are a denial of wisdom. Wisdom demands a new orientation of science and technology toward the organic, the gentle, the nonviolent, the elegant and beautiful. Peace is indivisible—how then could peace be built on a foundation of reckless science and violent technology?" wrote Schumacher.

It was for peace, sustainability, and the well-being of people and the Earth that Schumacher advocated small-scale organizations: he believed they will always be less harmful to the natural environment and less likely to lead to war than large-scale ones.

Schumacher knew even small communities can be guilty of destruction and aggression, but because of their limited scale and power he recognized that their impact will also be small in comparison with the negative impact exerted by gigantic groups or nations motivated by power, profit, and greed. If there was any evidence that bigness will be accompanied by humility, modesty, and restraint, then he would have had no objection to large-scale operations, corporations, and nations. But that, he believed, is not the case.

Having been through the experience of working with large organizations, Schumacher saw that big organizations make their judgements on a very narrow basis and these judgements are biased toward the short term—quarterly balance sheets or the annual profit margin. Transnational corporations seeking global markets depend on the infrastructure built by governments with taxpayers' money, and yet they are able to employ clever accountants to avoid paying taxes. Moreover, their financial calculations exclude the true cost to the environment.

In addition to narrowness and short-termism, large economic institutions encourage irresponsible individualism; they are not concerned with spiritual, social, and environmental well-being. They will consider it uneconomic, for example, to give preference to locally produced goods if imported goods are cheaper. Market forces, free trade, globalization, and economic growth put together have created the "religion of economics" where the reign of quantity triumphs. Schumacher wrote, "When economic thinking is based on the market, it takes the sacredness out of life, because there can be nothing sacred in something that has a price." In such a system, even simple non-economic values like beauty, health, or cleanliness can survive only if they prove to be "economic."

Buddhist Economics

Schumacher was invited by the Burmese government to advise them on developing their economy on the Western model. In 1955, he spent nearly six months in Burma visiting villages, towns, temples, and monasteries and talking to wise elders. He soon realized that the Burmese had a perfectly good economic system of their own, which he called Buddhist Economics. At that time, he could see that ordinary Burmese were contented, creative, and close to nature, happily caring for the land, animals, and people. Of course they could develop a few intermediate and appropriate technologies to ease their work, but why should an industrial, urban, and mechanized system be imposed on them?

> *Good work is not to be confused with chores or drudgery. Good work and good living complement each other. Good work improves the quality of life and brings well-being.*

SATISH KUMAR

It became clear to him that replacing such a traditional economy with a modern, Western-style economy would lead to more problems than solutions. He realized that Buddhists see "the essence of civilization not in a multiplication of wants but in the purification of human character." And that character is partly formed by good work and the dignity of labor. For Schumacher, work was not merely a job, an occupation or employment. It was a source of creativity, imagination, and spiritual growth; "Work properly conducted blesses those who do it and equally their products," wrote Schumacher. Through good work, what Buddhists call "Right Livelihood," human beings are transformed for the better, and through bad work they are changed for the worse.

Therefore society has an obligation to encourage good work and to value its artisans, artists, craftspeople, farmers, gardeners, builders, and traders. The industrialization of work and mass production diminishes the opportunity for good work and for the "purification of human character." Good work is not to be confused with chores or drudgery. Good work and good living complement each other. Good work improves the quality of life and brings well-being.

Buddhism is not "antagonistic to physical well being," Schumacher wrote. "It is not wealth that stands in the way of liberation but the attachment to wealth; not the enjoyment of pleasurable things but craving for them. The keynote of Buddhist economics, therefore, is simplicity and nonviolence." A Buddhist economist would say that "Since consumption is merely a means to human well-being, the aim should be to obtain the maximum of well-being with the minimum of consumption . . . and [since] physical resources are everywhere limited, people satisfying their needs by means of a modest use of resources are obviously less likely to be at each other's throats than people depending upon a high rate of use. Equally, people who live in highly self-sufficient local communities are less likely to get involved in large-scale violence than people whose existence depends on worldwide systems of trade." Moreover, "To satisfy human wants from far away sources rather than sources nearby signifies failure rather than success."

Thus Schumacher called his discovery of Buddhist economics a "homecoming." Schumacher found abhorrent the idea that the industrialization of agriculture is development and living by the land and obtaining a livelihood through small-scale agriculture with the help of craftwork and human-scale trade is underdevelopment. The pursuit of pure materialism, for Schumacher, was a dead end. On the other hand, integrating Buddhist principles of a small, simple, and nonviolent way of life with principles of sound economies would facilitate a spiritually, socially, and ethically resilient society. He came to the view that his task and that of his generation was one of "metaphysical reconstruction."

This conviction was not merely an emotional response. It was based on intellectual and empirical evidence that modern industry swallows so many natural resources while accomplishing very little. Schumacher wrote, "An industrial system which uses 40 percent of the world's primary resources to supply less than 6 percent of the world's population (of the rich countries) could be called efficient only if it obtained strikingly successful results in terms of human happiness, well-being, culture, peace, and harmony." It was self-evident to Schumacher that the economically developed countries like the USA and Europe had not achieved the desired success in environmental sustainability, social coherence, or human happiness, whereas a country like Burma, which had a flourishing democracy at that time, and was mostly agrarian with thriving craftsmanship and adherence to the Buddhist principles of simplicity and nonviolence, was much happier and less demanding of natural resources.

Schumacher was one of the rare economists from the Western world who saw the intrinsic link between economics and ethics. Buddhism for him was a metaphor for moral and spiritual values. He wanted society to follow the direction of nonviolence rather than violence, cooperation with nature rather than destruction of her, low-energy solutions rather than brutal, wasteful, and clumsy solutions of fossil-fuel-driven, nuclear-power-based industrial societies. Schumacher was convinced that a way of life based on materialism and limitless economic expansion in a finite environment cannot last long.

Explaining his view of a Buddhist economics, he wrote that it "would make the distinction between 'renewable' and 'non-renewable' resources. A civilization built on renewable resources, such as the products of forestry and agriculture, is by this fact alone superior to one built on non-renewable resources, such as oil, coal, metal, etc. This is because the former can last, while the latter cannot last. The former cooperates with nature, while the latter robs nature. The former bears the sign of life, while the latter bears the sign of death. It is already certain beyond the possibility of doubt that the 'oil-coal-metal-economies' cannot be anything else but a short abnormality in the history of humankind. The New Economics would be a veritable 'Statute of Limitation'—and that means a Statute of 'Liberation.'"

Again and again, he emphasized that "economics is not an exact science; it is in fact, or ought to be, something much greater: a branch of wisdom." He concluded that life, including economics, is worth living only if it is an unpredictable, unfolding, emerging process and a pilgrimage.

Schumacher's Pilgrimage

Schumacher began his own pilgrimage by escaping from Nazi Germany in 1937. While his brother-in-law Werner Heisenberg, the quantum physicist, decided to stay in Germany, Schumacher, who had been a Rhodes scholar at Oxford University, declared that the fight against Nazism could only be conducted outside Germany. So he came to live in England. But as fate would have it, he became an alien suspect and therefore was interned. Then his friend David Astor, the owner and editor of the *Observer* newspaper, offered him a house on his land and some work on the farm. This was the beginning of his journey of deep appreciation of and affinity with the natural world. He felt totally at ease working with his hands, cultivating the soil, caring for animals, and being out in nature—be it wind, rain, or snow. Here was an Oxford economist getting his hands dirty in the soil, which eventually led him to becoming the president of the Soil Association and campaigning for organic agriculture and tender loving care of plants, trees, animals, and all living creatures.

Eventually he acquired a four-acre garden in Caterham, south of London, and devoted himself to the growing of vegetables, herbs, flowers, and fruit trees. His love of silviculture made him a keen advocate of the regeneration of forests. His film *On the Edge of the Forest* was a profound statement of the unity between nature and humankind. He firmly believed that in order to cultivate respect and reverence for nature, it is important to shift our consciousness from ownership to relationship. We do not own land, forests, animals, or rivers; we are merely temporary custodians of the natural resources under our care. We must recognize their intrinsic value. Our duty and responsibility is to take care of them without polluting, depleting, or exhausting them.

"An ounce of practice is worth more than a ton of theory," he said. And he practiced what he preached: he was a conservationist, an ecologist, and a protector of wildlife. But above all he lived his ideals in his everyday life.

His farmer friend Sam Mayall, also a member of the Soil Association, supplied him with organically grown wheat. "I want to know exactly where my food is coming from," Schumacher said. He had a small flour mill to grind his flour. He baked bread every week for the family. Fruit, vegetables, and herbs came from his garden, which he cultivated with profound devotion. He fed the soil with compost he had made. He believed that "if you take care of the soil, the soil will take care of the rest."

Schumacher was the head of statistics at the UK National Coal Board and a member of a highly scientific and intellectual family. Yet he was attracted to Buddhism, environmentalism, baking, gardening, windmills, and solar power. This was in the 1960s and 70s, when such things were considered fringe and flaky. People found him rather odd. They called him a crank. Schumacher retorted, "What's wrong with being a crank? A crank is a small and simple tool which causes revolutions." His book *Small Is Beautiful* proved revolutionary; it revolutionized the hearts and minds of millions.

Schumacher's Legacy

In 1973, as Schumacher's book was in the process of being published, I was offered the editorship of *Resurgence* magazine by its founder, John Papworth. I was in two minds: to accept or not to accept the honor. While I was talking to Schumacher about it, he spotted my hesitation.

"What's the problem? You will be an excellent editor," said Schumacher.

"But I would like to go back to India," I said.

"Why?"

"I would like to continue working with the Gandhians."

"Satish, there are many Gandhians in India; we need one in England—so why not accept this offer and make *Resurgence* a voice of Gandhian philosophy in the West?" he asked.

This was a very persuasive argument. My hesitation melted away.

"Alright, I will accept the editorship on your advice, but I will need your support. Will you undertake to write an article for every issue?" I asked.

"Okay, that's the deal," was Schumacher's reply.

I was delighted. Schumacher kept his promise until he died in 1977. His thirty-five *Resurgence* essays are now published as a collection, entitled *This I Believe*.

> *Schumacher firmly believed that in order to cultivate respect and reverence for nature, it is important to shift our consciousness from ownership to relationship.*

SATISH KUMAR

Four years of working relationship with Schumacher developed into a profound friendship. After I received his article, I would call him and talk about it. Often, we discussed ideas and themes for the magazine as well as philosophy, politics, religion, and much more.

When Schumacher died, I felt that although he had passed away physically, his vision and values would continue to inspire generations to come. I saw it as a sacred responsibility to keep his vision alive, develop it further, and bring it to the attention of the public in general and the environmental movement in particular.

With this commitment and passion, I called a meeting of a number of his friends and environmentalists and we established the Schumacher Society (1977), Annual Schumacher Lectures held in Bristol (1977), The Small School in Hartland (1982) for education of children aged eleven to sixteen years, the Human Scale Education Movement (1983) to support small innovative schools, and eventually, in 1991, Schumacher College for the study of ecological and spiritual values and for transformative learning.

Thus the work and legacy of Schumacher in the UK is flourishing. Similar societies were established in the United States, Germany, and India. The work of the Intermediate Technology Development Group, of which Schumacher was the founder, is going from strength to strength under the new name Practical Action, operating in many countries at the grassroots level, promoting tools for sustainable, holistic, and ecological development. Similarly, the work of the Soil Association, of which Schumacher was the president, is a continuous expression of this approach to land and farming. The work of the New Economics Foundation, the Centre for Alternative Technology, and Friends of the Earth is bringing Schumacher's approach into the arena of policy and influencing the political landscape in the UK and around the world. *Resurgence* magazine, now merged with *Ecologist*, is the flagship publication of Schumacherian philosophy, articulating a holistic vision through art, poetry, and essays on politics, economics, ecology, and ethics.

With the world facing acute global crises such as global warming, global poverty, global debt, and a moral vacuum, the simple solutions proposed by Schumacher may be our salvation; think small, go local, and act from a high moral ground. This is what Schumacher meant by metaphysical reconstruction. The time is ripe; the time is now. Let us take up the challenge.

7

New Paradigm vs. Old Paradigm

In the new paradigm, Earth is Gaia, a living organism, a biotic community, a self-regulating, self-sustaining, living system.

Soil, Soul, Society is a trinity for a new paradigm. We need to shift from the old paradigm of fragmentation, dualism, disconnection, and division to a new paradigm of wholeness, connectedness, and relatedness.

In the old paradigm, the economy is based in the principle of linearity: take, use, and waste. In the new paradigm, the economy will be cyclical, as in nature: take with gratitude, use sparingly, replenish what is taken, and put back what is left over into the earth as compost—no waste, no pollution, and no depletion.

In the old paradigm, economic growth is pursued at all costs. In the new paradigm, growth in the economy has no significance. What matters is growth in well-being and happiness. A country like Bhutan, where gross national product (GNP) is being replaced by gross national happiness (GNH), is an example of a step toward a new paradigm.

In the old paradigm, development directed toward the poor takes the form of aid or charity, but in the new paradigm we look at the causes of poverty and work toward social justice and solidarity. In the old paradigm, development is introduced from outside: economists and politicians look at the poor and say, "You need a road, you need a hospital, you need a school, you need industry, so we will bring people from outside and build them for you and you pay us in rents, insurance, tolls, and taxes."

In the new paradigm, outsiders withdraw their control and ownership of local resources and respect local tradition, culture, wisdom, medicine, and all other ways of life so that the local community is enabled to stand on their own feet and develop from the inside out. If outsiders sincerely and genuinely wish to help, they become part of the local community, live within the community, and find their livelihood from the same sources as the local community.

In the old paradigm, attention is paid to increasing living standard and to the provision of cars, computers, and other consumer goods. In the new paradigm, what matters is quality of life, not the quantity of possessions. What is important is health, creativity, culture, craft, food, family, friendship, mutuality, and time to be, rather than the continuous struggle to have.

In the old paradigm, bigger is better. Big dams, big factories, big corporations, big business, big military, and big government. In the new paradigm, small is celebrated—it is not size but substance that is valued.

> *In the new paradigm, small is celebrated—it is not size but substance that is valued.*
>
> SATISH KUMAR

In the old paradigm, cities are centers of progress. Highrise tower blocks, glamorous banks, seductive casinos, and tempting shopping centers are considered symbols of civilization. In the new paradigm, a culture of agriculture, care for the countryside, integrity of rural communities, appreciation of the role of market towns, conservation of nature, and the renewal of craftsmanship and artisanal modes of production are supreme.

In the old paradigm, machines dominate, mechanization is better than manual work, progress is measured by the amount of work done by machines, every problem is expected to have a technological solution, and every human need has a technofix. In the new paradigm, there is dignity in human labor. Serving, making, producing, building, gardening, cooking, and umpteen other human activities have intrinsic value. The machine is an aid to human hands, not a replacement of them. The machine is welcome as a tool, as a servant, but not as a master.

In the old paradigm, monoculture leads the way. Chain stores dominate every high street. The same brands, the same clothes, the same foods, the same restaurants are available everywhere. The same architecture rises up in cities around the world. In the new paradigm, cultural diversity as well as biodiversity are central to social organizations and human settlements. Local distinction in all aspects of life is paramount. Local cheese, local wine, local craft, local foods, local dress, local music, local dance are encouraged, promoted, and preserved, all while respecting and learning the cultures of other countries.

In the old paradigm, globalization is the backbone of trade. Countries specialize in a few products and export them around the world to service the global economy. In the name of comparative advantage, competition is encouraged. Mergers, takeovers, and monopolies favor the strong and powerful and penalize the weak. Social Darwinism—survival of the fittest—rules the market and governs international trade. In the new paradigm, small and local is preferred. Trade is not only for the exchange of goods and maximization of profit, it is also a way of enhancing human relationships, and interdependence is celebrated as a way to foster friendship. Instead of globalization, localization ensures environmental sustainability and the resilience of the local community.

> *In the new paradigm, the principle of subsidiarity is observed diligently. People at the grassroots are trusted to conduct and manage their own affairs. Central organizations restrict themselves to business that requires central decision.*
>
> SATISH KUMAR

In the old paradigm, decisions are handed down from the top as if people at the top know better. Rules and regulations are made, laws passed, taxes collected, and justice meted out from the capital of the nation, where parliaments, supreme courts, the civil service, and headquarters of banks and businesses are located. In the new paradigm, the principle of subsidiarity is observed diligently. People at the grassroots are trusted to conduct and manage their own affairs. Central organizations restrict themselves to business that requires central decision. Otherwise, local communities are empowered to decide for themselves how to manage health, education, policing, taxation, transportation, and necessary activities.

In the old paradigm, the reductionist scientific method is the only way of knowing, the sole source of truth. If something cannot be measured, analyzed, and defined, there is a tendency to think that it does not exist. In the new paradigm, there are many ways of knowing, including the scientific way. Intuition, religion, feelings, mythology, and storytelling are given equal status to reason. In addition to empirical knowledge, indigenous vision is also respected. "Science without religion is blind and religion without science is lame." So said Albert Einstein. The new paradigm is holistic and inclusive.

The old paradigm is mechanistic; Earth is compared to a machine and considered to be inanimate and dead matter. In the new paradigm, Earth is Gaia, a living organism, a biotic community, a self-regulating, self-sustaining, living system.

The old paradigm is dualistic, as defined by René Descartes and followed by most, if not all, scientific and educational establishments. In that dualism, mind is separate from matter and mind rules over matter. The new paradigm is non-dualistic. Mind and matter are one and inseparable. Quantum physics is the physics of the new paradigm, where there is no distinction between the observer and the observed.

> *All beings are interrelated and bound together through common evolution and a common origin. All people share a common humanity.*
>
> SATISH KUMAR

The old paradigm is hierarchical, whether the class system of the West or the caste system of the East. These systems are steeped in the idea of superiority and inferiority. Businesses work within the framework of bosses and workers. Religious orders have popes and priests, ayatollahs and mullahs, gurus and disciples. People suffer under hierarchies of color, race, and gender. All beings suffer from speciesism. The new paradigm is based in networks: all beings are interrelated and bound together through common evolution and a common origin. All people share a common humanity. The Earth is a web of life and a biotic community.

The old paradigm is about control, whether through the power of the military or money or knowledge. Controlling others is ingrained in education, in governance, and in economic systems. Rulers want to be in control, and they are afraid of losing control. The new paradigm is based on the concept of participation. People participate in the process of life. They go with the flow. They accept what is and whatever emerges. They are open to the unfolding phenomena of human imagination, creativity, and nature's ever-changing forms and patterns.

Such a new paradigm is built on the foundation of Soil, Soul, and Society.

8

The Benevolent Universe

There is a world soul, anima mundi, of which we are an integral part. A soul that is cared for brings us joy and happiness.

We live in a benevolent universe. The soil is the most benevolent. It provides conditions for a seed to germinate, to be born, to grow, to realize its potential. It is the soil that holds the roots of a tree for as long as the tree lives so that the tree can remain strong and spread its branches into the sky, receiving energy from the sun, enabling photosynthesis.

The benevolence of the soil is endless; it helps one single seed to multiply into millions of seeds for hundreds of years, producing colorful, aromatic, juicy, and delicious fruit, feeding birds, bees, humans, and animals. The tree celebrates the benevolence of the soil and becomes benevolent in return, offering its fruit to whoever is in need, without condition and without judgement, a sinner or a saint, a poet or a prisoner, a prince or a peasant. The tree gives wood to fashion a chair, a bird a branch to make her nest, and oxygen to maintain life.

The benevolence of the sun is beyond the capacity of words to describe. It burns itself to maintain life; it makes the Earth and all beings upon it move. The sun ripens the crops to feed all beings, humans and other-than-humans alike. It provides conditions for photosynthesis for the whole plant kingdom to nourish itself and give nourishment to bacteria, insects, birds, and animals.

The moon is benevolent. It maintains the cycle of life and cycle of time. Time and tide are sustained by its presence. The moon is the patron saint of poets and painters and an embodiment of feminine principles.

Rain is benevolent. It emerges from the ocean, riding in the chariot of clouds, delivers itself to every farm, field, forest, mountain, and human habitat, free of charge, without needing any external supply of energy. It moistens the soil, quenches the thirst, fills rivers, ponds, lakes, and wells and, in partnership with the sun, it feeds the world.

Fire is benevolent—it is in our belly, it is in our hearth, it is there to purify, to heat, to light, to cook, to digest, to decompose, and to liberate; even a forest fire is a source of regeneration. In our ignorance and anger we may misuse fire power, but the challenge is to subdue ignorance and anger and develop right relationship with the power of fire. The benevolence of fire is of a different order to the benevolence of soil and sun; nevertheless, fire is benevolent, and without it there can be no life.

> *If you look at the world with benevolent eyes, the world reciprocates with benevolence.*

SATISH KUMAR

Air is benevolent. We breathe, therefore we are. Air is related to the spirit, to inspiration, to spirituality; all creatures are sustained by the same breath of life. Air is breath of Brahman, breath of the universe, breath of God. In Sanskrit air is *prana*, which means life itself. In Chinese air is *chi*, which means the source of energy. We are blessed when we have a breath of fresh air. Our clothes and homes are renewed when they are aired. Lack of air causes stuffiness. Air is eternal and truly benevolent.

Space is benevolent. All and everything is held in space and by space. All movements, all changes, and every kind of dynamism are sustained in the stillness of space. We always need to be mindful of reducing our clutter and maintaining spaciousness in order to be detached and free.

Soul is benevolent. Compassion, kindness, generosity, and inner luminosity are the qualities of the soul. Mind, intelligence, and consciousness are held in and processed by soul. Soul is the seed of life. Feelings, emotions, sentiments, intuition, and reason pass through soul and manifest in the world. It is soul that holds memory. It is not only humans who have soul; animals, birds, insects, and microbes have soul. Soil, trees, rocks, and rivers have soul. Even a home has soul. A soulless house is no good to live in. There is a world soul, *anima mundi*, of which we are an integral part. A soul that is cared for brings us joy and happiness.

Society is benevolent. Each and every one of us together make society, the human community. Language, culture, literature, arts, architecture, agriculture, knowledge, science, and much more are all created by society and shared among humanity. We pay no royalty to speak in English or French, Sanskrit or Chinese. Myths and legends, plays and poetry are handed down from generation to generation, orally and in writing. Without society there is no civilization and no culture. Even strangers are benevolent to strangers and offer hospitality. The healthy help the sick, the young help the old, the rich help the poor; there is benevolence all around.

We have inherited wisdom from the indigenous peoples. We have received religion from the great masters like Muhammad, Mahavira, Moses, the Buddha, Jesus Christ, and Lao Tzu. What we have gained through the long history of humanity is measureless. We are indebted to society, which we cannot pay back, nor is any payment demanded of us.

Families are benevolent. We are born of love. Our parents loved each other, embraced each other, and conceived us in love. Our mother gave us the security and safety of her womb and carried us in her belly until we were ready and strong enough to embrace the world. The benevolent universe puts milk in our mother's breast so that we can be nourished with the love of our mothers. Our fathers, uncles, and aunts kept their benevolent eyes on us to ensure our healthy upbringing. Our parents worked hard to provide for us everything we needed and much more and gave us a sense of responsibility so that we might share our love with our children to ensure the continuing benevolence.

Doctors are benevolent, nurses are benevolent, teachers are benevolent, taxi, train, and bus drivers are benevolent. It is thanks to them that we can visit our friends and family, attend our daily business, and carry out our responsibilities.

The world is how you see it and what you make of it. If you look at the world with benevolent eyes, the world reciprocates with benevolence. If you project suspicion and self-interest, you get the same in return. Trust begets trust, and fear begets fear. Recognizing the benevolence of the universe is not to deny the shadow side, but seeing nature as red in tooth and claw and people as selfish and greedy makes us respond in a similar vein. If we sow seeds of malevolence, malevolence will grow; if we sow seeds of benevolence, benevolence will grow.

A traveler was passing through a village and asked someone standing by, *"What's the next village like? Is it friendly?"*

The person asked in return, "How was the village you have just come from?"

"Oh, it was awful; people there were unfriendly and indifferent, some even hostile," said the traveler.

"The next village is similar," was the reply. So the traveler walked on with an anxious frown.

After a while another traveler stopped to ask the same question, "What's the next village like?"

The same person replied with the same question, "How did you find the previous village?"

This time the response was different. "Oh, it was good; people were friendly, helpful and hospitable," said the traveler.

The person in the village replied, "You will find the next village similar."

If you project benevolence, you will get benevolence in return. This is the moral of the story, and we all understand it easily when we hear such a story. But when it comes to racial, religious, or national conflicts, we lose our confidence and play a different role.

In spite of the innate nature of human kindness, the world faces multiple conflicts. Palestine versus Israel, Iran versus the USA, and India versus Pakistan are some of the conflicts that have been with us for more than sixty years, and there seems to be no light at the end of the tunnel.

Let us suppose that the leaders of the USA say to the government of Iran, "We wish to be your friends; we have no desire to undermine your national interest and no desire to interfere in your internal affairs. We will never do anything to harm your people. We will sell our goods to you at a fair price and buy your oil at a fair price and never use military force against you. In addition, we will progressively reduce our stockpile of nuclear weapons. If there are any disagreements between our two nations, we will negotiate with you through the UN and other diplomatic channels. Fear us not. We wish to treat you as our equal."This would be a statement of benevolence.

Then suppose the government of Iran says, "We never wish to harm the national interest of the USA. Nor will we attack Israel. Let us sit down together and never stop negotiating until we find a fair resolution and a just outcome for fellow Muslims—the Palestinians. They have suffered long enough. Now the time has come to offer them terms and conditions that are fair and just. We will use only peaceful, nonviolent means to solve our problems." With such statements of benevolence, it will be impossible for either the USA or Iran to engage in threats, ultimatums, suspicions, and boycotts.

Similar statements of benevolence could be exchanged with genuine conviction and sincere belief between any party in conflict. Often, behind a veil of diplomacy lie threats and ultimatums, suspicion and distrust. Nations spend billions and billions of dollars and pounds and see their young men and women mutilated in war, but they are reluctant to use the language of trust and kindness. Benevolence is a simple and effective way to resolve all conflicts immediately or in time, whereas war begets war, suspicion begets suspicion, and hatred begets hatred. We have seen it throughout history, but we refuse to learn from history. Politicians, militarists, and traders in arms have blind faith in the power of the gun and the bomb, even though in the end only negotiations succeed. Politicians are compelled to negotiate after they have exhausted themselves, be it in Vietnam or Ireland.

Apartheid ended through benevolence. The Berlin Wall came down and satellite states of the Soviet Union became free through the benevolence of Mikhail Gorbachev and other enlightened Russian leaders. The European Union came into being after centuries of strife, thanks to the foresight, wisdom, courage, and benevolence of the promoters of the Treaty of Rome. Colonialism ended in many countries through negotiation rather than violence. Slavery came to an end because many slave owners started to listen to their conscience and found it morally abhorrent to own other human beings. Racial discrimination in the United States became illegal through nonviolence and the benevolent struggle of civil rights leaders like Martin Luther King.

> *Since the history of benevolence is so successful, there is no logic or reason not to embrace it.*
>
> SATISH KUMAR

Since the history of benevolence is so successful, there is no logic or reason not to embrace it. But some people call me naive and unrealistic. Then what have the realists got to show for their efforts? What have the realists achieved? Millions dead in wars. Millions dying of hunger and starvation. Millions of people homeless and jobless despite abundant resources of nature, a tremendous amount of technology, and trillions of dollars and pounds whizzing around the world every minute. If this is what realists are able to achieve, then what is so good about being a realist? Under the watch of so-called realists, oceans are overfished and polluted, the biosphere is saturated with greenhouse gases, and our population is exploding beyond the carrying capacity of the Earth. If this is the achievement of realists, then now is the time to say goodbye to the realists and give idealists a chance.

However, the idealists need to build a movement of benevolence. At the moment there are benevolent individuals and benevolent organizations but no movement as there was against slavery and against apartheid. The Soil Association, Friends of the Earth, Greenpeace, WWF, RSPB, CPRE, the National Trust, and similar organizations concerned with the countryside and conservation of the soil and nature are mostly working in isolation from spiritual and social justice groups. Similarly, faith groups, New Age groups, and Yoga and meditation centers focus narrowly on care of the soul and personal development, while organizations working for social justice such as Oxfam, the World Development Movement, and Médecins Sans Frontières are only fighting their corner. The movement for environmental justice, social justice, and spiritual renewal are three aspects of benevolence. If they all came together and worked together, there would be a strong movement for transformation, for change, and for the creation of a new paradigm.

I am not arguing that organizations merge; in fact, it is good to maintain their organizational identities and yet develop a common manifesto for the ideals of environmental sustainability, spiritual fulfillment, and social justice. By joining hands, they will be in a stronger position to influence policy makers, business leaders, the media, academia, and the general public. If they stand side by side and work together, their strength and influence will rise tenfold: 1 + 1 = 11.

We need to create a movement of benevolence and nonviolence—by example, by argument, and by practical action.

It is not that we can build a utopia of benevolence where malevolence is eradicated, but we need to challenge the institutionalizing of malevolence in the form of militarism, materialism, consumerism, and sectarianism. A small amount of narrow individualism and self-interest can be dealt with, but when malevolent institutions take control and benevolence is relegated to the personal sphere, then we are in danger of losing our way and jeopardizing the well-being of people and planet.

The leadership for benevolence will not come from the prime ministers or presidents of the world, and a culture of benevolence will not be legislated through parliaments and senates. Such leadership and such culture have to emerge from the grassroots. Therefore, individuals and organizations committed to the care of the soil, qualities of soul, and concern for society need to work together to build a grassroots movement.

Such a movement has to work at two levels. The first step is to challenge and resist malevolent institutions engaged in damaging the integrity of the Earth, undermining spiritual values, and perpetuating social injustice and economic exploitation. In the past, such resistance was offered by the champions of social and political liberation such as Mahatma Gandhi, Martin Luther King, Nelson Mandela, and Aung San Suu Kyi. Exposing the folly of institutionalized violence is necessary to wake people up, but then the second step is to build alternatives, develop new models, and create institutions that promote organic farming, animal welfare, protection of wildlife, conservation of rainforests, respect of all faiths and support of interfaith dialogue, release of political prisoners, nuclear and general disarmament, promotion of cooperatives, and encouraging conflict resolution through peaceful means. The list of such a constructive program is inexhaustible. There are many wonderful projects already in existence, but they lack the political and financial muscle to punch above their weight.

This two-pronged approach is essential for building a powerful movement for personal, social, and environmental transformation. This can be achieved only when we are able to rise above our personal and organizational egos. We have to move from ego to eco; from g to c. Ego is all about personal success, personal power, and personal recognition, whereas eco is about communities—Earth communities as well as human communities. Eco is about relationships; eco entails collective success and collective well-being.

The public awareness about environmental sustainability, quality of life, and social justice has risen by leaps and bounds in the last fifty years since the publication of Rachel Carson's book *Silent Spring*. In the 1960s, concern for renewable energy in the form of solar and wind power was very much a minority interest. Animal welfare and vegetarianism was also a small movement. The idea of development was all about aid and charity, the westernization of the global south, and the industrialization of agrarian societies.

Now we are living in a different world. Evidence of global warming and depletion of fossil fuels has woken people up. The membership of environmental organizations is greater than the membership of political parties, so there is cause for optimism and hope. The industrial monoculture and systems of mass production are as the blink of an eye when set in geological time. Civilizations have come and gone. The structures of imperialism and colonialism are severely diminished. There is no guarantee that the fossil-fuel-dependent, anti-nature, globalized economy will last; it is already showing signs of fatigue. What is created by humans can be changed by humans. We need to build a movement with all the courage of our convictions.

Every government in the West is struggling to sustain economic growth. The ideal of full employment has become unrealizable. Trust in politicians and the media is at an all-time low. Personal fulfillment and job satisfaction has also become elusive. Industrialized societies are in the grip of a spiritual crisis as much as an environmental and economic crisis. Bankers do not know how to manage money, politicians do not know how to make peace, economists do not know how to create employment. The consumer society is in confusion. Therefore, the time is ripe for a big change. Environmental, spiritual, and social movements need to seize the opportunity and show that another world is possible, a world where nature is respected, where compassion and cooperation are valued, and where people come before profit. We can initiate and implement the great transition from a capitalist economy to an ecological economy and value natural wealth above financial wealth. Money and finance have a place, but we must put them in it and not allow them to dominate our entire way of life.

This holistic vision, where natural, spiritual, and social dimensions are brought together into an integrated reality, is an urgent necessity. We have to see the whole elephant and not this or that part, as the six blind men did. According to the story, six blind men encountered an elephant. One touched the trunk, the second came in contact with the tusk, the third felt a leg, the fourth touched the ear, the fifth felt the stomach, the sixth held the tail. They all thought they knew what an elephant was. When the elephant was gone, they started to exchange their impressions of the elephant.

"I know an elephant is like a huge cobra, long and sinuous," said the first blind man.

"No, no, you've got it wrong. It is hard and smooth and pointed like a carved stone," protested the second blind man.

"Not at all," interjected the third blind man. "The elephant is like a pillar, round and tall."

"You, too, have got it wrong, my friend," said the fourth blind man. "The elephant is flat and thin, like a fan."

"I am sorry to say that none of you has got it right," argued the fifth blind man. "It is large and round, like the bottom of a big vessel."

"No, no, no! I held the elephant, it is like a thin, supple, and strong rope," said the sixth blind man.

They quarreled and were about to come to blows when a passerby stopped at the commotion of the blind men. When he heard what they were talking about, he laughed and said, "Stop, stop, you fools! The cobra-like part of the elephant is the trunk, the stone-like part is the tusk, the fan-like part is one ear, the pillar-like part is the leg, the vessel-like part is the belly, and the rope-like part is the tail. All these parts together make the whole elephant."

"Thank you, thank you, gentleman. Now we understand and now we get it."

This parable of realization shows that we may all have a part of the solution, but we need to know the big picture in order to build an effective movement. And that big picture has an ecological dimension, a spiritual dimension, and a social dimension encapsulated in the trinity of Soil, Soul, Society.

SOIL,
SOUL,
SOCIETY

An article written by
Satish Kumar in December 2022

Most of our present problems are a consequence of our separational world view. We see nature and humans as separate, soul and body as separate, matter and spirit as separate, subject and object as separate, and within human community we see separation and division in the name of race, religion, nationality, and political philosophy. This world view is based on an outdated Newtonian physics that considers nature as a machine and Earth as a dead rock. The Cartesian dualism of mind over matter has also contributed to the separational paradigm. Now we are in the age of a new science of entanglement, interdependence, Gaia, and quantum physics, where all things exist in relationship with each another and Earth is a living organism.

The new path to a better world is to heal the wounds of division, disconnection, and separation. We need to see the unity and interrelatedness between nature, spirit, and humankind; we need a trinity representing the unity of life, the trinity of Soil, Soul, and Society; we need a trinity for a new paradigm, a trinity of relational world view, a trinity to upshift our consciousness; a trinity to launch a new movement of connectedness to make peace with the Earth, peace with the self, and peace among people of diverse cultures and backgrounds. Peace within and peace without. Inner peace and outer peace.

Many historical movements in the world have three key words that express their spirit. During the French Revolution, for example, the key words were *liberté, égalité, fraternité*, and in the United States Declaration of Independence we find the words "life, liberty, and the pursuit of happiness." *Liberté, égalité, fraternité* is a very nice trinity, but it is very human: human liberty, human fraternity, human equality. In the same way, in the United States Declaration of Independence, life is human life, liberty is human liberty, and happiness is human happiness. These words represent an anthropocentric world view. We have come to think that somehow human beings are separate and yet at the center of the universe. It is as if humans are the most important species and the Earth's other species are all there to serve humankind. Not only is this a human-centered world view, but it also sees humans as apart from the rest of nature.

But in the age of Gaia this world view is out of date, especially once we realize that we are utterly dependent on and connected with other species. We need to recognize that humans are not the rulers of the world; they are not here to do what they like. It is our responsibility to take care of the other species because we are all made of each other, we are not separate, we are all related, we are members of one Earth community. The animals, birds, forests, oceans, and mountains are our ancestors. We all have come from a single source, a single origin.

So we need a new trinity to replace those human-centered trinities. (Even the trinity adopted by the New Age movement, "mind, body, spirit," refers to the human mind, human body, and human spirit.) We need a new trinity that is holistic and inclusive, a trinity that embraces the well-being of the entire planet Earth and not just the well-being of human species. We need a philosophy, a science, a religion, and a legal system that recognize the intrinsic value of all living beings, not just the well-being of humans.

For this reason, I propose a new trinity. And at the top of this new trinity, I put the word "Soil," which represents the entire natural world. Without soil there is no food, and without food there is no life, no trees, no forests. Food and forests are transformed soil. Soil represents life on Earth. In our human-centered world view, in our educational systems, and in our study of science and technology, we have come to think that soil simply means dirt, and that dirt is dirty. But dirt is not dirty: dirt is the source of life. Without dirt there is no life.

Soil, therefore, represents all natural life. It is a fact that we are related to and dependent on the soil. Some people may think that food comes from the supermarket; most of us don't grow food these days. If somebody grows food, we think: "Oh, poor man, peasant, laborer; he is not educated, so he has to grow food." We think if you are educated, then you don't grow food. Growing food in the Industrial Age has no dignity. You sit behind your computer, and your food comes from some faraway places. You don't want to grow food, because growing food is seen as a sign of backwardness. If you are advanced, educated, rich, and smart, then you manufacture cars or computers or some other gadget or you become a banker, a lawyer, or a civil servant. Production of food is increasingly left to robots, computers, and other machines.

Growing food has become a sign of underdevelopment. The word "peasant" has become a term of insult. We need to change that. We need to say that we must touch the soil; we must put our hands into the soil. How many times do we touch our mobile phone every day? Maybe a hundred times? How many times do we touch the soil? Hardly ever! We need to give dignity to peasants, to those who grow food, to farmers and gardeners.

Soil is so important, yet we have forgotten it. Yes, we humans are important too, but the human species is only one of the 7.8 million species on Earth. We are not the kings. We are not an imperial power, and the Earth is not a human colony. At the moment we behave as if we can do to the Earth what we like. We do things that cause global heating and change the climate, we poison the soil, we destroy the rainforests, we overfish the oceans and fill them with plastic, we interfere with seeds through genetic engineering. We treat animals cruelly in factory farms. These are acts of war on nature! We engage in such a war because we see ourselves as separate from nature. This human behavior must urgently change to move toward a better world, a peaceful world. We need to realize we are nature, we are all an integral part of this healthy web of life maintained by soil in particular and by nature in general. As we are nature, what we do to nature we do to ourselves.

We need to be humble; to be human is to be humble. The Latin word *humus* means "soil." "Human," "humility," and "humus" all come from the same root. Human beings are literally soil beings. There is no separation between humans and humus. The soil is so important, yet humble. When humans lose humility, they are no longer true humans. Seeing humans as separate and above soil, above nature, is a sign of arrogance.

Once, the Buddha was sitting in meditation, with his right hand above the palm of his left hand, and his son, Rahul, came to him and asked: "Father, you teach compassion, forgiveness, love, and forbearance—where did you learn all these wonderful qualities? You are a world teacher, but who is your teacher?" The Buddha lifted his right hand in the bhūmisˊpara mudra, which means "touch-the-earth posture" and he touched the ground. Then he said: "I learned my forgiveness, compassion, friendship, kindness, and all the other wonderful qualities of love, beauty, unity, and generosity from the Earth."

Do you know where the Buddha was enlightened? Sitting under a tree. My mother used to say that the Buddha got enlightenment because he was sitting under a tree!

A tree has intrinsic value; a tree is good, but not because it gives us food, wood, shade or aesthetic pleasure. No, the tree is good in and of itself, even if nobody goes and looks at it, even if nobody ever says: "Wow, look at those beautiful cherry blossoms!" Even if no one ever sees it, the tree will still blossom. Trees represent divine grace appearing on the Earth. Trees, animals, plants, rocks, mountains, rivers, worms, butterflies, honeybees—all creatures upon this Earth—have intrinsic value. They have the right to be as they are, who they are, and what they are. We talk about human rights, and that's fine. But nature also has rights. The trees have a right to exist. We have no right to cut them down without proper purpose. When we understand this, when we recognize the rights of the trees, the rights of nature, then we are truly ecologists and have understood the paramount importance of the word "soil." Recognizing the integrity and the sanctity of the soil is the first essential step toward a better world, a sustainable and regenerative world. This is a step toward making peace with the Earth.

The second word in this new trinity is "Soul," which sounds similar to "soil." Soil has soul. Trees have soul. Everything is soulful, yet soul is something we cannot see. The body we can touch, hug, kiss, and admire, but in order to touch soul we have to close our eyes. Soul is something we can only experience. Trees, animals, worms, and humans—all have a soul. Soil is the outer landscape, and soul is the inner landscape.

We need to take care of the soul, as we take care of the body. But we can only take care of the soul when we slow down. No computer. No car. No shopping. Just sit in your room with tea and flowers: elegantly simple, without clutter. Go into a room that is peaceful. Take no mobile phone. Take time for yourself. Meditate on the fact that you represent the totality of the universe. There is nothing in the universe that is not in you, and there is nothing in you that is not in the universe. The universe is the macrocosm, and you are the microcosm. You are earth, air, fire, water, imagination, creativity, consciousness, time, and space—you have all these elements in your genes and in your cells. Your soul is billions of years old. You have been recycled and recycled, again and again. You are a beautiful example of the total recycling principle of the universe.

So if you want to take care of the universe, you start with yourself. Care of the soul is the way to self-realization. Meditation is for self-realization, as is gardening: mindful gardening is a form of meditation. When you are cooking mindfully you are also in meditation because you are not just cooking to feed yourself or your family, but also for self-realization. Taking care of yourself, being at ease with yourself, being happy with yourself, being fulfilled in yourself is the way to self-realization. Whoever I am, I am. Self-realization makes you at ease with yourself. Everything you truly need and want is within you; courage, compassion, creativity, and consciousness are all within you. You are capable of solving every problem in the world with your inner wisdom. Wisdom is a soul quality, as are generosity, love, friendship, unity, and beauty. We are all gifted with these qualities. They are there to be cultivated and manifested.

You will realize that all you need is already here: air, fire, food, water, trees, soil, sun, and sky, everything is here. What more do you want? If you want more possessions and more clutter, it is because you have lost touch with your soul. That's why your soul is hungry. That hunger will not be satisfied by computers, cars, or mobile phones. To nourish the soul, you need to slow down and take care of your soul. Without a happy soul you are the poorest of the poor. Spiritual poverty is the greatest poverty, greater than any physical poverty. And as you take care of the soil, you take care of the soul. Your outer body is soil, and your inner being is soul. When you take care of both body and soul, you experience a sense of the sacred, you gain self-realization, and you achieve true well-being.

Caring for the soul has nothing to do with our ego. This is why we have the third word of our trinity: "Society." First and foremost, we are members of the Earth community. Then we are members of the human community. This sense of belonging to the human community liberates you from ego!

I walked from India to America without money. When I came to the border between India and Pakistan—where three wars have been fought—I was joined by thirty-five people who had come to say goodbye. One of them said: "Here are some packets of food. At least take some food with you." I said: "Thank you, but no thank you. I'm going for peace. And peace begins with trust: trust in human community. These packets of food are not packets of food. They are packets of mistrust. What would I tell my Pakistani hosts? That I did not trust them to feed me?"

My friend began to cry. I said: "Why are you crying, my friend?" She replied: "Satish, this might be our last meeting. I may never see you again. You are going to Muslim countries, Christian countries, capitalist countries, communist countries, mountains, forests, deserts, snow. You have no money, no food. You are walking. How are you going to survive?" At that moment, I said: "My friend, from today on I'm not afraid of death. If I die walking for peace, that is the best kind of death I can have. I'm not afraid of hunger. If I don't get food, I'll say this is my opportunity to fast."

Then we entered Pakistan, and to my astonishment there was someone waiting for us. He said: "Are you the two men coming to Pakistan for peace?" I was surprised. "How do you know?" I asked. He said: "I read about you. And I thought that if you are coming for peace, then I should welcome you. This war between India and Pakistan is complete nonsense. We are all members of one human family."

At that moment, I realized the fundamental unity of the human family. If we come as Indians, then we will meet Pakistanis. If we come as Hindus, then we will meet Muslims. But if we come as human beings, then we will meet human beings. This way I was able to rise above my narrow identity and identify myself instead with the whole of human society.

Mahatma Gandhi said that there is enough in the world for everybody's need but not enough for anybody's greed. At the moment, 1 percent of the greedy population are driving the economy, while 99 percent of people are suffering. This 1 percent of the population want to be the superpower and dominate the world. For them there is no such thing as society. But for peace, justice, and happiness, we need to embrace the whole of society. We need to solve social problems of poverty and wars with imagination, creativity, and forgiveness. All human problems can be solved by negotiation, by friendship, by letting go of ego, and by going into eco. Eco means home, eco means relationships. Let us make a shift from ego to eco, from self-interest to mutual interest, to the common interest of the whole human society.

If we can have a holistic trinity of Soil, Soul, and Society, if we can understand the interdependence of all living beings and understand that all living creatures—from trees to worms to humans—depend on each other and that we are all gifted with human spirit, then we can live in peace and harmony with ourselves, with other people, and with nature. That is why I present you this new trinity of Soil, Soul, and Society.

A MEDITATION ON THE UNITY OF LIFE

Let us bring both our palms together,
And bow to sacred life, sacred soil, sacred Earth, sacred
universe.
We see all beings in us, and ourselves in all beings.
We see the whole universe in ourselves, and ourselves in the
whole universe.
Each one of us is a microcosm of the macrocosm.
Cosmos is our country,
The planet Earth is our common home,
Nature is our nationality,

And love is our religion.
All living beings are sustained by the same breath of life.
Thus we are all connected, we are all related, we are
*   interbeings.*
We all share a single origin.
Unity and diversity dance together.
All thriving is mutual.
When separation and divisions end, suffering ceases.
We go beyond right and wrong, beyond good and bad.
We bow to the unity of life. We bow to the diversity of forms.
We bow to the sacred, to life, to the Earth, to the universe.
Breathe in. Breathe out.
Smile, relax, and let go.
Let go of all expectations, attachments, and anxieties.
Let go of all worries, fears, and anger.
Let go of ego,
And let us move from ego to eco.
Breathe in. Breathe out.
Smile. Relax. Let go.
We are at home. I am at home. I am at home. We are at
*   home.*

SATISH KUMAR

GRATITUDE

This book would not have been possible without the help and support of June, my wife. Most mornings we have non-domestic conversations over a cup of tea when old ideas are revisited, new ideas are explored, and some tentative conclusions are crystallized. These meandering conversations flow freely. They come and go most of the time, but some of them stayed in my thoughts and resulted in this book.

Moreover, June has been most generous with her time and participated in this process of writing, critiquing, and revising. No words can do justice to express my deep gratitude to June for her attention and engagement.

Also I would like to thank profusely Lee Cooper, my friend of forty years, who has typed the handwritten manuscript meticulously. Lee, June, and I started to work together on *Resurgence* magazine in 1973. Ever since, Lee has been, and still is, a pillar of strength.

My heartfelt thanks go to Elaine Green, who has been working with me and assisting me with my writings for over a decade now. Her selfless support is invaluable in putting the final shape to this book.

And my deep appreciation goes to Monica Perdoni, who inspired and encouraged me to write this book in the first place. Editing *Resurgence* and *Ecologist*, teaching at Schumacher College, and fulfilling my public speaking engagements leave very little time to write a new book. But it is Monica's friendship and persuasion that have enabled me to set some time aside and put these words on paper. So, thank you, Monica!

BIBLIOGRAPHY

Bhave, Vinoba. *Talks on the Gita*. Pavnar, India: Paramdham Prakashan, 2017.

Dyson, Ketaki Kurshari, trans. I *Won't Let You Go: Selected Poems by Rabindranath Tagore*. Hexham, UK: Bloodaxe Books, 2010.

Paranjape, Makarand R. *Acts of Faith: Journeys to Sacred India*. Carlsbad, CA: Hay House, 2012.

Parel, Anthony, ed. *Gandhi: "Hind Swaraj" and Other Writings* (Cambridge Texts in Modern Politics.) Cambridge, UK: Cambridge University Press, 2009.

Schumacher, E. F. *Small Is Beautiful: Economics as if People Matter*. London: Vintage Books, 1993.

The Tagore Centre. *Purbi: A Miscellany, Correspondence between Tagore and Leonard Elmhirst*. London: The Tagore Centre, 1991.

Tagore, Rabindranath. "A Poet's School," essay in Rabindranath Tagore and Leonard Elmhirst, *Pioneer in Education. India:* Visva Bharati, 1961.

Wood, Barbara. *Alias Papa: A Life of Fritz Schumacher*. Oxford: Oxford University Press, 1985.

ABOUT THE AUTHOR

A former Jain monk, SATISH KUMAR is an international peace and environmental activist and the long-standing editor of the highly respected *Resurgence* magazine. In 1962 he hit the headlines and gained international respect for his 8,000-mile peace pilgrimage to London, Moscow, Washington, and Paris. He is the founder of the Schumacher College, which educates its students in ecological consciousness and the means for effective change. He lives in the UK.

INDEX

Monastics and visitors practice the art of mindful living in the tradition of Thich Nhat Hanh at our mindfulness practice centers around the world. To reach any of these communities, or for information about how individuals, couples, and families can join in a retreat, please contact:

PLUM VILLAGE
33580 Dieulivol, France
plumvillage.org

LA MAISON DE L'INSPIR
77510 Villeneuve-sur-Bellot, France
maisondelinspir.org

HEALING SPRING
MONASTERY
77510 Verdelot, France
healingspringmonastery.org

MAGNOLIA GROVE
MONASTERY
Batesville, MS 38606, USA
magnoliagrovemonastery.org

BLUE CLIFF MONASTERY
Pine Bush, NY 12566, USA
bluecliffmonastery.org

DEER PARK MONASTERY
Escondido, CA 92026, USA
deerparkmonastery.org

EUROPEAN INSTITUTE OF
APPLIED BUDDHISM
D-51545 Waldbröl, Germany
eiab.eu

THAILAND PLUM VILLAGE
Nakhon Ratchasima
30130 Thailand
thaiplumvillage.org

ASIAN INSTITUTE OF
APPLIED BUDDHISM
Lantau Island, Hong Kong
pvfhk.org

STREAM ENTERING
MONASTERY
Beaufort, Victoria 3373
Australia
nhapluu.org

MOUNTAIN SPRING
MONASTERY
Bilpin, NSW 2758, Australia
mountainspringmonastery.org

For more information visit: *plumvillage.org*
To find an online sangha visit: *plumline.org*
For more resources, try the Plum Village app: *plumvillage.app*
Social media: *@thichnhathanh @plumvillagefrance*

PARALLAX PRESS, a nonprofit publisher founded by Zen Master Thich Nhat Hanh, publishes books and media on the art of mindful living and Engaged Buddhism. We are committed to offering teachings that help transform suffering and injustice. Our aspiration is to contribute to collective insight and awakening, bringing about a more joyful, healthy, and compassionate society.

View our entire library at parallax.org.

THE MINDFULNESS BELL is a journal of the art of mindful living in the Plum Village tradition of Thich Nhat Hanh. To subscribe or to see the worldwide directory of Sanghas (local mindfulness groups), visit mindfulnessbell.org.